"The stories will inspire you. The lessons will change you. Jay Payleitner shows twenty-first-century fatherhood for what it is and for what it needs to be."

—**Dr. Dennis E. Hensley**, professor and author of more than 50 books, including *Man to Man* and *The Power of Positive Productivity*

"I have been a wife for 37 years, a mom for 31, and a daughter for...well, let's just say even longer. With those credentials, I highly recommend this book to all dads. It is a good read and, more importantly, a *great* guide for any man desiring to meet the needs of the children God has entrusted to his care."

—**Kendra Smiley**, radio host, conference speaker, and author of *Be the Parent* and *High-Wire Mom*

"Jay Payleitner has given fathers a gift... a wise, delightful, practical, and profound book. If you're a father, you will thank him, and if you're not, you'll read this book with joy and give it to a father who will 'rise up and call you blessed.'"

—**Steve Brown**, seminary professor, author of *Welcome to the Family* and other books, and the "voice" of Key Life Network

"Moms of all ages, grab this book for your husbands! It's inspiring, encouraging, and easy to read."

—**Ellen Banks Elwell**, author of *The Christian Mom's Idea Book* and *When There's Not Enough of Me to Go Around*

"*52 Things Kids Need from a Dad* reminds all of us of the humbling privilege and exhilarating joy of fatherhood. You won't find any lectures or guilt trips here. Instead, it's more like 52 inspiring halftime talks. As your personal fathering coach, Jay will provoke you to think deep, laugh hard, and love more, leaving you with 52 unexpected fathering insights."

—**Carey Casey**, CEO of The National Center for Fathering, speaker, radio host, and author of *Championship Fathering*

"This is great stuff, worth any dad's time. If you can't benefit from this, you're not listening. Ignore it only if you don't want to be a better dad. The first three copies are going to my grown sons."

—**Jerry B. Jenkins,** coauthor of the megaselling LEFT BEHIND series and author of over 150 other published works

"Jay's chapter 'Kids Need Their Dad to Stop and Catch the Fireflies' is worth the price of the book. As my friend Philip the Firefly might say, 'Payleitner hits pay-dirt on lighting up a dad's heart!'"

—**Dr. Emmett Cooper,** author of *The HoneyWord Bible* for kids of all ages; founder and president of HoneyWord Foundation

52 THINGS KIDS NEED FROM A DAD

JAY
PAYLEITNER

HARVEST HOUSE PUBLISHERS

EUGENE, OREGON

Cover by e210 Design, Eagan, MN

Cover photo © Fancy Photography / Veer

Jay Payleitner is represented by MacGregor Literary.

52 THINGS KIDS NEED FROM A DAD
Copyright © 2010 by Jay K. Payleitner
Published by Harvest House Publishers
Eugene, Oregon 97402
www.harvesthousepublishers.com

Library of Congress Cataloging-in-Publication Data
    Payleitner, Jay K.
    52 things kids need from a dad / Jay K. Payleitner.
        p. cm.
    ISBN 978-0-7369-2723-9 (pbk.)
    1. Father and child—Religious aspects—Christianity. I. Title. II. Title: Fifty-two things kids need from a dad.
    BV4529.17.P39 2010
    248.8′421—dc22

                                                    2009031514

To my bride, Rita,
who makes me a better dad.
And to all wives
who do the same
for their husbands.

Contents

Foreword
by Josh McDowell

One of the great benefits of being in ministry more than 40 years is
that you get to see whether or not all the things you've been speaking
and writing about stand the test of time. Certainly the cultural climate has
changed drastically, but I'm pleased to confirm (and not at all surprised) that
truth is still truth, Jesus is still "more than a carpenter," and young people
still need unconditional love and strong role models.

In 1991, I co-authored the book *How to Be a Hero to Your Kids,* which
helped give a biblically based, positive parenting plan to a generation of fathers.
One of those young dads was Jay Payleitner, who was the producer for *Josh
McDowell Radio* for more than 13 years. During our marathon recording
sessions, we covered a wide range of critical topics, including apologetics,
teen abstinence, and international outreach, but some of our most impas-
sioned broadcasts focused on the responsibility fathers have to make building a relationship with their children a top priority.

A story I told more than once on radio reveals the single greatest secret
to being an awesome father. I cannot take any credit for it, except for the
fact that I was smart enough to listen, smart enough not to let my ego get
in the way, and smart enough to allow myself to be broken before God.

To put it in context, Dottie and I were living in San Bernardino, California. Kelly was four and Sean was two, so it was quite a few years ago.
Katie and Heather were not even born yet. I recall that I was in my study
on a Thursday afternoon at about 3:30. I was on a roll, writing a chapter of
a book to meet a deadline, when in wandered Sean.

"Want to play, Daddy," he chirped.

As an "experienced" parent, I should have realized that basically Sean just wanted a hug, a pat, and a minute or two to show me the new ball he was carrying. But I was working on something important and felt I just didn't have even two minutes right then.

"Son," I said, "how about a little later? I'm right in the middle of a chapter."

Sean didn't know what a "chapter" was, but he got the message. Daddy was busy and he'd have to leave now. He trotted off without complaining and I returned to my manuscript. My relief was short-lived. In a minute or two, Dottie came in and sat down for a "little chat." My wife never tries to nail me; she has much gentler—and more effective—methods.

"Honey, Sean just told me you were too busy to play with him. I know that this book is important, but I'd like to point something out."

"What is that?" I asked a bit impatiently, because now my wife was keeping me from my all-important project.

"Honey, you're always busy. You're a five-ring circus. You will always have a deadline to meet, a chapter to finish, a talk to prepare, and a trip somewhere to give it. But honey, you won't always have a two-year-old son who wants to sit in his daddy's lap and show you his new ball." Having made her point she started to walk out, but stopped, turned, and left me with words that cut into my heart and have stayed with me ever since. "You know, if you spend time with your kids now, they'll spend time with you later."

Not immediately, but about three minutes later I found myself on the carpet next to the desk. I made a pledge before God that I try to keep to this day. Until that moment, I had often made the shortsighted vow, "I will always put my family before my ministry." But that wasn't right. That wasn't God's plan for fathers. On my knees I said, "God, I never, ever again will put my family before my ministry." In that moment of brokenness, God made it very clear that Kelly, Sean, Katie, Heather, and Dottie do not come *before* my ministry. They *are* my first ministry.

I've shared that lesson in books, in front of thousands of men, on television specials, and on hundreds of radio stations. Right there in our recording studio, Jay must have been listening with an open heart, because I know for a fact that his family is his first ministry. Being a hero to his five kids is his absolute priority, and Jay continues to be an advocate and influencer for fathers across America.

So, Dad, let me reconfirm. Your kids need you. God does have a plan for fathers. The biblical fathering principles I first delivered decades ago are still valid and are perhaps more important than ever. I'm delighted to see so many inspiring, practical, unexpected ideas for dads in one place.

Finally, let me add one more spin to that lesson I learned from Dottie more than 30 years ago. "If you spend time with your kids now, you'll spend time with your *grandkids* years from now."

With three precious grandchildren always eager to spend time with their Papa Josh and Grandma Dot, I can personally attest to another of the great truths found in the book of Proverbs. "Grandchildren are the crown of old men, and the glory of sons is their fathers" (Proverbs 17:6 NASB).

—Josh McDowell
October 2009

A Lesson from Hollywood

Before we get started talking about dads, here's a simple little quiz for movie fans...

What is the 1986 movie *Top Gun* about?

What is the 1986 movie *Ferris Bueller's Day Off* about?

What is the 1994 movie *Forrest Gump* about?

If you said "a hotshot Navy pilot," "a streetwise teenager who ditches school to hang out in Chicago with his girlfriend and best friend," and "a simple-minded guy who accidentally experiences dozens of historic events," you would be wrong. All three movies are about fathers and sons.

Allow me to explain. About halfway through *Top Gun*, Tom Cruise as Lt. Pete "Maverick" Mitchell has an underplayed scene with his commanding officer, played by Tom Skerritt. In the scene, Maverick finally learns the circumstances of his father's heroic death and hears *this* insight from Commander Metcalf: "Yeah, your old man did it right. Is that why you fly the way you do? Trying to prove something?" Any filmgoer paying attention discovers that Maverick's most desperate need is not to shoot down Russian MiGs, bed down Kelly McGillis, or find forgiveness for Goose's death. What drives him is the need to reconcile himself with the loss of his father.

Despite what you may think, *Ferris Bueller's Day Off* was not about Ferris Bueller. The Matthew Broderick character didn't change, grow, or learn anything. The film is really about Ferris' buddy, Cameron, who is destined to cap off the eventful day by having a life-changing conversation with his father. With his dad's red 1961 Ferrari 250 GT California smoldering at the bottom of the ravine behind his house, there's no avoiding it. Like Maverick's father, the audience never meets Cameron's father, who "loves this car more than life itself."

We see the same aching for a father-child connection, but from a different perspective, in *Forrest Gump*. The iconic Tom Hanks character is not searching for reconciliation with his father—instead he is searching for purpose in his own life. Despite being a football hero, decorated war veteran, table-tennis champion, shrimping tycoon, and millionaire, Forrest literally and figuratively can't stop running. Only when he discovers he has a son and a namesake does his life make sense. The movie ends with big Forrest sitting on a stump after putting little Forrest on the school bus and reassuring him, "I'll be right here when you get back." A restless soul finally finds rest.

The relationship between fathers and their children is a classic movie staple. When the voice in the *Field of Dreams* cornfield whispers, "If you build it, he will come," it's talking about Kevin Costner's father coming to "have a catch." In *Armageddon*, Bruce Willis sacrifices his own life—not to save the world, but to save his daughter's boyfriend. *Footloose* is not about dancing teenagers, it's about John Lithgow overprotecting and finally learning to let go of his daughter. *Back to the Future*, *Rain Man*, *Sleepless in Seattle*, *It's a Wonderful Life*, *To Kill a Mockingbird*, *The Godfather*, *Elf*, *Superman*, *Batman*, *Hulk*, *Star Wars*, *The Little Mermaid*, *The Lion King*, *Finding Nemo*, and a zillion other blockbusters leverage father-son or father-daughter relationships to motivate the characters and drive the narrative.

Here's the point. Hollywood is in the business of knowing what topics resonate with as many people as possible. Studios spend a lot of money researching the best way to emotionally connect with their audience. Even if movie scripts go off the deep end and fill the heads of filmgoers with dangerous or ludicrous notions, movie producers are usually on the right track when it comes to knowing what topics trigger the emotional response of ticket buyers.

So Hollywood is well aware of the significance of fathers. How about you? Do you fully understand the power of a father's words and actions? Do you know that children are born with a kind of deficit or vacuum that only fathers can fill?

If you picked up this book to make your life better, that's perfectly acceptable. The Bible confirms that your relationship with your children can and should be a source of great personal joy.

> The father of godly children has cause for joy.
> What a pleasure to have children who are wise.
> —Proverbs 23:24 NLT

But maybe reading this book will have an impact beyond you and your family. As it turns out, the entire destiny of humanity depends on the "hearts of fathers." The last verse in the Old Testament clearly states that dads and kids need to make deep emotional connections. Otherwise, God is going to curse the land.

> He will turn the hearts of the fathers to their children, and the
> hearts of the children to their fathers; or else I will come and strike
> the land with a curse (Malachi 4:6).

No pressure, Dad. However, I'm thinking it might be a good idea to do everything possible to turn your heart to your sons and daughters, to be the kind of dad your kids need.

I promise, it's not a burden. It's a blast. The rewards come early and often. So pour your heart and soul into your children. Build a legacy. Have high expectations. Laugh and cry with your kids. Ask for God's grace to wash over your family. Be the dad. Be the hero. This is your chance to rescue the world and leave all those Hollywood fathers in the dust.

Kids Need Their Dad...

To Help Them Beat the Odds

Think of the top ten social crises of our time: Drug abuse. Teenage pregnancy. School shootings. Gangs. Spiritual confusion. Overcrowded prisons. AIDS and other sexually transmitted diseases. Domestic violence. Drunk driving. And so on.

We can make the case that the most devastating rips in our social fabric would be radically reduced if dads were getting the job done at home.

Statistically, what happens when dads aren't around?

- Eighty-five percent of all youths sitting in prisons grew up in a fatherless home.[1]

- Children who live apart from their fathers are 4.3 times more likely to smoke cigarettes as teenagers than children growing up with their fathers in the home.[2]

- Fatherless boys and girls are twice as likely to drop out of high school; twice as likely to end up in jail; four times more likely to need help for emotional or behavioral problems.[3]

- Seventy-five percent of all adolescent patients in chemical-abuse centers come from fatherless homes.[4]

- Three out of four teenage suicides occur in households where a parent has been absent.[5]

- Adolescent females between the ages of 15 and 19 years reared in homes without fathers are significantly more likely to engage

17

in premarital sex than adolescent females reared in homes with both a mother and a father.[6]

Sound hopeless? Just the opposite. If father absence is devastating, leading to all kinds of bad decisions and societal ills, then father presence is the solution, right?

This hard data, along with all kinds of anecdotal evidence, is rarely brought into the light. Even with all the research, too many segments of society express little regard for fatherhood. The media, school administrators, television scriptwriters, judges, church leaders, and state agencies seem to say fathers don't matter. Or they've given up on fathers. Or worse, we're told fathers are part of the problem. The result is, men are driven away from their families, fathers are disenfranchised, and dads are afraid to hug their own kids.

But the inverse is true and must be said. Men need to hear, "Dad, you matter!" "Your children need you." "Your wife (or the mother of your children) needs you to be more involved and more invested in the daily lives of your kids." Without strong male role models, families suffer both short- and long-term. Children make bad decisions. Communities weaken. Government agencies flounder to fix problems *after the fact*. Taxes go up. Our streets aren't safe. As soon as they graduate high school, young people turn their back on Jesus. The vibrant potential of the next generation is lost—in many cases, for eternity.

An oft-quoted survey found that if a mother attends church regularly with her children, but without their father, only 2 percent of those children will become regular church attendees. But if a father attends church regularly with his children, even without their mother, an astounding 44 percent choose to become regular church attendees on their own.[7]

Yes, dads matter. Do you want more proof?

All you have to do is ask a kid.

Takeaway

Just opening this book and reading this far proves you want to be the kind of dad your kids need. You can do it, Dad.

"I cannot think of any need in childhood as strong as the need for a father's protection."

SIGMUND FREUD (1856–1939)

Kids Need Their Dad...

To Stop and Catch the Fireflies

A friend of mine and I were reminiscing about growing up. He shared with me his single most vivid memory of his dad. You might think it would be some well-planned vacation or some expensive, extravagant gift. But it wasn't. You see, my friend's father was on the road a lot, a busy important man—things to do, people to see. Well, one evening this father and his eight- or nine-year-old son were driving. My friend could not recall the destination, but it was business-related. Clearly, it was someplace important and they were running late.

On a quiet stretch of two-lane highway, all of a sudden this dad pulls off the road. It wasn't an emergency-type stop. But my friend recalled that he was frightened for just a moment. The entire situation reflected the urgency of a flat tire, but there had been no galumphing sounds or shaky steering. Within seconds, this dad had hopped out of the car, rolled up his shirtsleeves, loosened his necktie, and opened the trunk. He didn't pull out the tire iron or a suitcase. Instead, he came around to the side of the car, tapped on the passenger window, and held up an empty glass jar. He motioned for his son to follow him and then—wingtips and all—he ran into the field...to catch fireflies. Lightning bugs. The field was full of them, and the hovering, dancing, flashing creatures blended into the clear starry sky. All told, that father and son weren't in that field very long at all. With their bare hands they caught scores of the bugs, letting most of them go. The dad poked some holes in the lid of the jar, the boy tossed in some grass because that's what you do, and he carried the jar back to the car like a trophy. The entire episode lasted less than ten minutes.

Now, we can never be sure what motivated that father at that moment to create the stuff of which memories are made, but we can speculate. Maybe the sight of those flashing insects just off the road had triggered memories of his own youth. Maybe he'd been carrying that jar around for months for just that purpose. Maybe, some heaven-inspired paternal instinct kicked in. Whatever it was, the lesson is clear: Dad, pull over to catch the fireflies.

Takeaway

Never miss a chance to stop and make a memory. Sometimes you may even want to orchestrate those moments yourself.

"A man's real possession is his memory. In nothing else is he rich, in nothing else is he poor."

—Alexander Smith (1830–1867)

Kids Need Their Dad...

To Carry the Calf Every Day

There's a story—I don't know how true it is—of a farmer's teenage son who wanted to build up his muscles. Old Bessie, the family cow, had given birth that summer, so the boy moseyed out to the barn and with little difficulty picked up that calf, put it on his shoulders, and walked three times between the barn and corn crib.

The next day, he did the same thing. And the next. And the next.

Of course, the calf was growing during this time. But as the story goes, since the boy could pick it up and take a short walk around the farmyard one day, he certainly should have been able to do it the next. After all, how much could one little cow grow in 24 hours?

You probably know where we're headed here. By the next summer, the boy was strolling around with an 800-pound full-grown cow on his shoulders, and he went on to become an Olympic clean and jerk gold medalist, NFL lineman, or something equally impressive.

The point? The point is that as parents, we need to get into the habit of spending time with our kids.

Allow me to apply the principle. How many of you dads can imagine yourselves hugging your teenage son in public? Hmm. Not many. Well, how many of you can imagine getting a great big hug from your kindergartner right in front of his classroom when you come to pick him up after the first day at school? Most of you...all of you.

If you can hug him when he's 5 years, 117 days old, can't you also hug him when he's 5 years, 118 days? Or 5 years, 119 days? And every day of the school year and beyond?

What's more, that kindergartener enjoys those hugs, needs those hugs, and begins to expect those hugs. What a wonderful security it is to be able to know that a hug is always waiting for you.

Similarly, it's easy to tuck in a four-year-old. You read a story, talk about the day, say a prayer, kiss them goodnight, and that's it. If you dedicate the right amount of time to it—say about 20 minutes—it can be a truly magical moment. With a little perseverance, a father can develop a bedtime ritual that continues until the day you drop them off at their college dorm. Over that 18-year span, the schedule will change, the topics of discussion will surely evolve, and you may miss a night or two. But if you are tenacious about tucking in your kids, you will build a connection with them that will last through the toughest times.

And by the way, that time together does more than make a positive connection—it actually protects your relationship from harm. For example, during any given day, you may have said some harsh words to your family. Your son may have disrespected his mother after school. Your daughter may be pouting over some unkind words said by a schoolmate. But at bedtime, the magical moments you've had over the years will help the walls fall down, and in the glow of the nightlight you can talk it out, trade apologies, put it all in perspective, and look forward to a new day.

Call it availability. Call it consistency. Our kids need to know they can count on us. They need to expect hugs, goodnight kisses, and other warm fuzzies over the long haul.

Takeaway

Practice persistent parenting.
Be there some way, every day.

> *"Nothing will take the place of persistence; talent will not: nothing is more common than unsuccessful men with talent. Genius will not: unrewarded genius is almost a proverb. Education will not: the world is full of educated derelicts. Persistence and determination are omnipotent."*
>
> —CALVIN COOLIDGE

#4

Kids Need Their Dad...

To Count the Train Cars

You're driving with a car full of kids. You're already late. And, of course, just as you approach the city's most notorious railroad crossing, the lights suddenly flash and the gates begin to swing down. Your adrenaline pumps and for one moment you consider flooring the gas pedal and squeezing under the descending black-and-white-striped barrier. Thankfully, good sense prevails and, instead, you jerk to a stop just as the world's longest freight train begins to slowly chug by. No damage. Everyone's alive. Still, all that bottled-up adrenaline has to go somewhere.

You have two options. The natural response is to scream, pound the steering wheel, wring it with your hands for good measure, mutter to yourself for a moment or two, and then sit quietly seething while 127 boxcars pass ten feet in front of you. That's one option.

The second option is to count cars. No...really. Think about it. Is a 127-car train good news or bad news? To a man of the world like you, who has seen and done everything, it's no big deal. But to that seven-year-old in your backseat, it's huge. As a matter of fact, once you reach 70 or so, he's yearning to break the magical three-digit barrier. You're wishing it was over, and he's wanting it to go on. Your little guy will carry the excitement of counting 127 cars for days.

And what are you doing while he's making railroad history? You're either grumbling or leading the count. Either cursing the lemons or making lemonade. Either teaching your children to be optimists or pessimists.

The fascinating thing about patience and self-control is not that it helps you to just survive setbacks. Surviving is easy. The truth is that patience and self-control help you take those occasional setbacks and use them for good.

Suddenly, a flat tire becomes a chance to teach your daughter a necessary life skill. A credit-card denial at the checkout line gives you a chance to reconsider an unnecessary purchase. A computer crash becomes a reminder that it's time to pause and consider what's really important.

There's a wonderful verse in the Bible that, regrettably, is quoted early and often when something horrible happens. "God causes everything to work together for the good of those who love God and are called according to his purpose for them" (Romans 8:28). Actually, that's the last thing someone wants to hear when the biopsy comes back positive or a pink slip shows up in the envelope with your paycheck. The verse is true, but that's not the point. When devastating events come your way, first you have to deal with the shock, anger, and denial. Much later you can begin to see a bigger picture in which everything truly does "work together for the good."

On the other hand, that verse can and should be referenced immediately when we stumble over one of irritations of everyday life. It's a reminder to "look for the silver lining." You might even play a little game with yourself and your kids. Acknowledge your frustration, but try to keep a smile on your face and figure out how to put a positive spin on the moment.

"That's pretty frustrating that we dropped the bag of groceries with the bananas on the bottom. Hey, let's try to find a recipe for banana bread."

"I can't believe we lost the television remote again. I think that might be a signal to play Monopoly or Scrabble."

"Why would the car dealership be closed? Well, maybe we can coax another year out of this clunker after all."

So, should dads actually look forward with a perverse sense of glee to long trains, smashed thumbs, bent sunglasses, and misplaced monkey wrenches? No, but it's nice to know that somehow, some way, it all works for the good.

Takeaway

Your kids are watching. So keep your cool.

Look for ways to turn a negative into a positive.

> *"Teach the older men to exercise self-control, to be worthy of respect, and to live wisely. They must have strong faith and be filled with love and patience."*
>
> —TITUS 2:2 NLT

5

Kids Need Their Dad...

To Start a File Folder with Their Name on It

Question, Dad: What do you do when your four-year-old proudly presents you with a drawing of what looks like a porcupine eating pizza on a piano on the porch?

Your first fatherly response is obvious. You *oooh* and *aaah*. Your second response is more calculated. Your next goal is to find out what is actually in the drawing without crushing their little creative spirit. Don't say, "What is it?" Instead invite the little artist up on your lap and say, "Whoa. This is most excellent. Tell me about it." Then start picking up on their verbal cues. Let them point to the indecipherable kayak, Ferris wheel, marching band, or wildebeest. Ask them open-ended questions that get them thinking and explaining. "How did you choose these two colors?" "These lines are straight and these are curvy. Why did you choose that?" The idea is to partner with them in the discovery of their own creative abilities and help them see how they have control over the creative choices they make. You can point out elements of their artwork that are bold and decisive, even suggesting that their efforts have led you to think new thoughts. Let them know that—like all the great works of art—their masterpiece has given you a new perspective on life, the world, or some other grand concept.

Finally, after the creative brainstorming session is over, the budding Picasso jumps down and says "You can keep it, Daddy."

Uh-oh—now what?

Certainly you say, "Thank you so much." But then you need to figure out what to do with it. If you tape or pushpin it to the wall, it will stay there for a very long time. Trust me, even now I'm looking at a silly moustache man made from pencil shavings, an orange-crayoned sports logo, and a computer-generated "King of the World" award that should have been taken down from the walls of my office long ago.

One option would be to convince the young artist that it would be "a perfect gift for mom!" Problem solved. Another option would be to post it on the fridge...which would also make it mom's problem. If it's truly delightful, you may want to have it professionally mounted and framed. (That's a rare occurrence, but with the right piece of artwork, suddenly you've got a forever keepsake.)

The best option is for you to accept it graciously and save it efficiently. On the back with pencil put the date and the artist's name, then slide it into your child's personalized file folder and drop it into your home filing cabinet. What if you don't have a file folder with your child's name on it? Make one. Don't have a filing cabinet? Get one or pick up a cardboard banker's box at your local office-supply store.

When the artist comes back three days later inquiring about the whereabouts of the work of art, you can honestly say, "I saved it!" And even pull it out as proof. Of course, this whole art-saving system only works with two-dimensional pieces. For sculptures, mobiles, woodworking projects, hats, masks, and models you'll need an alternate (and perhaps more ruthless) system.

Once you've established a personalized file folder for each of your kids, you can also use it as a bonus receptacle for all kinds of memorabilia. What else can you shove into a 9 x 12 file folder? Report cards, concert programs, math quizzes, school awards, team rosters, notes they left for you, notes you left for them, newspaper clippings, Father's Day cards, movie tickets, menus, and memorabilia from any adventure you share over the years.

Just to clarify. This isn't the place for critical medical records, current sports schedules, or precious photographs. This file folder is a catchall for stuff you just don't know what to do with.

When you come home from an outing with a program in your pocket, suddenly you have a place for it. Your child's name is printed on it, so you don't want to throw it away, but you also don't want it cluttering your kitchen counter or credenza. Just slip it in the file folder.

Be warned, when that folder gets about an inch thick it will contain more than a few minutes worth of memories. So don't pick it up and start leafing through it unless you have plenty of time to let the years of memories wash over you.

──────────────── **Takeaway** ────────────────

You can't stop time. You can't save everything. But it's astonishing how one photo, one phrase, one tangible reminder of the past can transport you back to a moment in time you thought was gone forever.

"God gave us memories that we might have roses in December."
—James M. Barrie (1860–1937)

Kids Need Their Dad...

To Kneel or Stand by Their Bed As They Sleep, Watching, Praying, Appreciating the Gift of Our Children, and Thinking About the Meaning of Love

You would die for your kids. I know that because I'm a dad just like you, and I would easily give my life for Alec, Randall, Max, Isaac, or Rae Anne. No question about it.

But in the busyness of life, we forget. We're distracted by the ongoing cacophony of the day.

That includes changing diapers, stepping on Happy Meal toys, trying to remember how to do long division, vacuuming Cracker Jack from your car seats, misplacing your cell phone, going out for a gallon of milk at 11:30 at night, worrying about the impact of the casino or strip club opening on the edge of town, signing report cards that could have been better, handing out $20 bills on demand, cleaning baby puke off the shoulder of your best sport coat, and wondering how hard you should push your kid to make first-chair violin or first-string shortstop.

Okay, so life as a dad is filled with challenges—large and small. Still, being a dad is a pretty good gig. Those creatures you call children are worth the effort, and with any luck they'll give you a million times more joy than frustration.

With that in mind, the purpose of this chapter is twofold.

First, to put down in words the depth of feelings that fathers have when

29

they really stop and think about their kids. The love. The humbling responsibility. The hope that each of our sons and daughters experiences a rewarding future of dreams realized and passions fulfilled. Our own desire to guide, but not control, their destiny. Taking pride in their successes and, maybe, just a little bit of the credit. The overwhelming emotion that comes when we consider the generational connection between our grandparents and our grandchildren—who will never meet on this earth but have a link through our own existence.

All that to say, I recommend that you sneak into your child's bedroom tonight and say a prayer of gratitude for the privilege of raising each son and daughter. If they're babies, be extra quiet. If they're grade-school age, reach down and touch their warm red cheek. If they're in high school, don't be surprised if they open one eye and say, "What are you doing in here?" (Go ahead and tell them that you're praying for them.) If they're away at college, in the military, or finding their own way in the world, stay a little longer and pray extra hard.

There's power when a father prays purposefully for his children.

Abraham prayed for Isaac. David prayed for Solomon. Zacharias prayed for his son, John the Baptist. The Bible teaches, "The prayer of a righteous man is powerful and effective" (James 5:16). Which, of course, serves as another reminder that we men need to get right with God in order to be responsible leaders for our family.

Which brings us to the second purpose for this chapter. When you stop and consider how much love you have for your children, you are getting just a glimpse of how much God loves you. As our heavenly Father, God loves each of us supernaturally and unconditionally. What's more, when God saw that mankind was sinful and had fallen short of his glory, he provided his only Son, Jesus, to pay the price for our sins.

Do you get it? God loves you even more than you love your children.

Takeaway

One of the great privileges reserved for fathers is that, when we look at our own children, we get just a small sampling of God's love for each of us.

"God showed his great love for us by sending Christ
to die for us while we were still sinners."

—ROMANS 5:8 NLT

Kids Need Their Dad...

To Catch Them in a Lie

You need to hope that your four-year-old looks you in the eye and tells you a flat-out lie. Actually that's not something you really have to hope for, because it will happen. That's what four-year-olds do. At a certain age, every child begins to realize that their world is not absolutely congruent with mommy and daddy's world. It dawns on them that sometimes you're not in the same room. Sometimes details escape mom and dad's attention.

Mom didn't notice when I forgot to brush my teeth. I dumped a handful of french fries behind daddy's car seat, and he didn't make me go back and pick them up. I scratched the coffee table with the can opener and the world didn't come to an end.

Suddenly they realize you may not be aware of everything they think, do, and say. Indeed, they become conscious of the concept that they may be able to "get away with stuff." Don't panic, Dad—this is actually a good thing. Realizing they are individuals separate from you is part of that process of discovering and trying out their independence. Taking a long-term view, independence is the goal. We want our kids to learn independent thinking so they move out sometime before their thirtieth birthday. However, knowing you have the *ability* to lie and *choosing* to lie are very different.

That first lie told by a three-, four-, or five-year-old is a landmark. It's a moment of huge consequence during which a moral code begins to take shape. It's a fork in the road for any individual. Please don't miss it. Don't laugh off their little fib as a cute, inconsequential phase. Don't be too tired to discipline your child that day. Hope that you and your wife are not on a two-week cruise while your youngster discovers and perfects his new ability to deceive adults by practicing on his soft-hearted grammy or scatterbrained aunt. Actually, you may not want to schedule too much time away from a child who may be heading toward that first prevarication. It's that important.

Let's consider the scenario. Your kid does something naughty. Not malicious. Just something that happens when a four-year-old is out of your sight for six minutes. Sissy draws on the wall with her new Crayola markers. The twins put your cell phone in the microwave. Timmy shaves the cat. You know they did it. No doubt about it. They even look guilty.

You ask what happened. Timmy says, "I don't know." You ask, "Did you shave the cat?" Timmy says, "No." You rephrase the question: "Did you cut the hair off Weeblefester's back?" Then Timmy either gets panicky or defiant. But he still says, "No."

This is all good news! You've caught them in the act. Dad, this is your chance to help them choose the right path from this day forward.

How do you respond? This is not a time to yell or spank or send them to their room. You are dealing with a crime of intellect. So use yours. Make a speech. A nice long speech. Something like this:

"Oh, Timmy. This makes me so sad. Shaving the cat is a bad idea. You shouldn't shave the cat. But that's not what makes me sad. What makes me sad is that you lied to me. I asked, 'Did you shave the cat?' and you said, 'No.' You didn't tell Daddy the truth. You lied to me. And you cannot do that. Oh my goodness, lying is a bad, bad thing. It's worse than shaving the cat. It's worse than teasing your sister. Timmy, look at me. You cannot lie. You must not lie. If I ask you a question, you have to tell me the truth. This is important. You want to know how important? A long time ago, God made a list of the ten rules. He called them the Ten Commandments. One of those rules was 'Do not lie.' That's one of God's most important rules. 'Do not murder' and 'Do not steal' are also on that list of rules. You wouldn't kill someone, would you? You wouldn't take something that wasn't yours, would you? It's the same with 'Do not lie.' It makes God sad. It makes me sad. Do you understand? This is a big deal. I need you to promise me that you will not lie to me ever again. Do you know why? Next time I ask you something, I need to know for sure that Timmy is telling the truth. Timmy would not lie to me. I can trust Timmy. Son, I love you. You love me. I know that for sure. But I also need to know that when you tell me something, it is true! Does this make sense? Do you understand? This is very important. You know what? I don't really care that you shaved the cat. That was just a silly idea you had and I know you won't do it again. I know you're sorry for shaving the cat. But please tell me that you will never lie to me or lie to mom ever again."

The goal here is for your son or daughter to be blown away by the importance of telling the truth. At this moment in time, they may see a whole new side of you. That's okay. Your over-the-top, repetitive emphasis of the need to obey the eighth commandment should leave them a little stunned. Don't be loud, be sincere. Make sure to emphasize that *you know they lied to you*. Done right—with most kids—that's all it takes. They literally might not lie to you again for the rest of their lives. Which, of course, is an entirely different set of problems. At some point down the road, you may *not* want to know what they've been up to. But that's another chapter.

Of course, this confrontational approach to parenting needs to be reserved for just the right moment and just the right purpose. If you try this with a toddler, they will think you're yelling at them. The concept of truth telling versus lying is beyond their comprehension. If you try this with a middle-schooler, they might look you in the eye and say, "Oh, Daddy, I will never lie to you again." And, that's already a lie. Middle-school kids who didn't learn this lesson early are some of the best liars around. But catch a child red-handed in a lie at just the right age, and you will be doing them a great service that will last them for the rest of their lives.

Takeaway

Kids are going to test you. Be ready. It is much easier to get them on the right track early—when their spirit is receptive and they have not yet learned to outsmart you.

"A false witness will not go unpunished, and he who pours out lies will not go free."
—Proverbs 19:5

8

Kids Need Their Dad...

To Tell Them the Hamster Died As Soon As the Hamster Dies

I actually overheard a mom boast about the trick she uses to get her kids to wear their seat belts. She tells them the car won't start until they are all buckled up. To be clear, she doesn't say, "I won't start the car." She says, "The car won't start," and then proves it by pretending to turn the key.

Yikes. What happens in a few years when her children find out their mom has been lying to them all that time? And what's next? The TV won't work unless your room is picked up? If you get out of bed in the middle of the night, the snakes under your bed will bite your ankles?

Another couple I met would tell their children they were "going to work" every time they left the house. Apparently, the little ones were not okay with mom and dad going out to dinner and a movie.

Dad, you can't lie to your kids just to make your life easier. That seems like common sense, but apparently lying for convenience is a way of life for much of our population. Maybe it's a product of too much TV-watching. I know that lying and lying to cover up lies is a frequently used scriptwriting device. It's funny when Laura lies to Rob about the scratch on the car or Theo lies to Cliff about getting his ear pierced. Frasier Crane, Michael Scott, George Costanza, Charlie Harper, and so on get away with all kinds of mendacity and prevarication. But life is not a sitcom.

How about the concept of withholding the truth to spare your child's feelings? That may sound like something you can justify, but it's dangerous territory. A lie is a lie. If grandma is going to the hospital for surgery, don't hide it. Explain it in terms your kids will understand. If your household income takes a hit and suddenly you can't afford cable TV or a big family vacation, tell your teenagers right from the start. They'll appreciate your honesty, and besides, they'd figure it out anyway. If the hamster dies, for heaven's sake do not buy a replacement hamster and try to pass it off as Buttercup or Nibbles. The kids will know! Even if they don't, you're establishing a precedent you can't afford to set. And, if you've got bad news, don't wait. The longer you avoid the truth, the harder it is to speak it.

There really shouldn't be any doubt about this concept. It bears repeating: Telling the truth is one of the Ten Commandments. (By the way, don't confuse lying with misdirecting the guest of honor to cover up a surprise party or keeping alive the legend of Santa Claus.) When a father lies it's especially unfortunate because—as with so many other character traits—if you do it, they'll do it too.

Staying committed to telling your kids the truth may also force you to come to terms with the reality of the situation you're facing. Sometimes when we lie to the kids, we may also be lying to ourselves. But to keep our families strong, we can't afford to be in denial about our finances, our health, or our family relationships. Allow honesty and integrity to shed light on any challenge you face. Answers are clearer when you meet them with straight-on honesty.

In the short term, the truth can be burdensome, and no parent wants to load their kids down with unnecessary worry, but truthfulness and transparency build trust and bring a family together. Hypocrisy, lies, and half-truths build walls that are difficult to bring down.

Oh yeah, my deepest condolences on the death of your beloved hamster.

Takeaway

Don't let your kids lie. And don't you lie either.

"Once the toothpaste is out of the tube, it's hard to get it back in."
—H.R. HALDEMAN (1926–1993)

9

Kids Need Their Dad...

To—Sometimes—Make an Illegal U-Turn on the Expressway and Drive 30 Miles Back to the Restaurant Where Your Son Left His Dodgers Cap

I'm thinking about the phases kids go through. When my oldest, Alec, was about five, it was the cartoon character He-man and his archenemy Skeletor. Being good parents, we bought him some He-man action figures. Not all of 'em, but a few.

Then there was this fascination he had with Los Angeles Dodgers pitcher Orel Hershiser. Not a bad role model. Orel was unashamed of his Christian faith, and as MVP of the 1988 World Series was invited on *The Tonight Show with Johnny Carson*, where he sang four lines from a hymn to millions of late-night viewers.

By the following summer, Alec had about 100 Orel Hershiser baseball cards and wore a Dodgers baseball cap everywhere he went. On a family vacation, he accidentally left that beat-up blue cap at a greasy-spoon diner we had stopped at for breakfast. By the time Alec realized it, we had traveled some 30 miles. At the time, I wasn't happy about it, but I made an illegal U-turn on the expressway and drove back to retrieve it. Only because it was that particular blue LA Dodgers cap. We had dozens of ball caps, but that one was important to Alec. So it was important to me. Which I guess is the point. Dad, if it's important to your kids, it should be important to you.

Getting down on your knees and playing with action figures, dressing up for a tea party, listening to bad clarinet, listening to music that doesn't sound like music, ogling sparkly rocks found at the beach, waiting outside a dressing room at Gap, memorizing the names of dinosaurs, driving them to just the right skateboard shop, saving your loose change for a coin collection, hunting down a mint condition rookie card of a favorite ballplayer. These are worthy endeavors. Mostly because it gives you a chance to enter your child's world and see things from their perspective. It gives you an awareness of who they are, what motivates them, and how to nurture their gifts.

This also explains why I drove Randy and his best friend, Bryan, to Cleveland for the 1998 DeLorean convention when they were 15. I even asked John DeLorean to pose for a photo with my son. That trip still provides mental images to which I can return anytime just for the sheer amusement. More than a decade later, I'm pretty sure Randy has moved on from his DeLorean phase, but in that season of his life I made the right choice to join him right in the middle of it.

Yes, phases and fascinations come and go. There will come a time when you bring home that long-coveted, limited-edition Pez dispenser and they aren't super excited, or excited at all. That just means it's time to figure out their next phase. Sooner or later that "phase" is going to lead to high-school extracurricular activities, a major in college, a fulfilling career, and maybe some hobbies or ministry work that brings a little more life to their life. When that time comes, Dad, you will share in that adventure because— since they were rug rats—you took seriously their hobbies, interests, quirks, passions, and curiosities. No matter how trivial or mundane or trendy or unorthodox, you knew it had great importance.

Takeaway

If it's important to your kids, it should be important to you.

"Praise God from whom all blessings flow,
Praise Him, all creatures here below,
Praise Him above, ye heavenly hosts,
Praise Father, Son, and Holy Ghost. Amen."

"THE DOXOLOGY" (1674), THOMAS KEN (1637–1711)
SUNG BY OREL HERSHISER ON *THE TONIGHT SHOW WITH JOHNNY CARSON*, 1988

#10

Kids Need Their Dad...

To Spy on Them

Don't let your kids read this chapter. DON'T LET YOUR KIDS READ THIS CHAPTER. They don't need to know all your secrets. Now, because my five kids will eventually read the following paragraphs, I may have to deliver this concept in dad-to-dad code, but I have a good sense you're smart enough to read between the lines.

One of your primary jobs is to know everything possible about your kid. Where they are. Who they're with. Their favorite subject. Their toughest challenge. Their best friend. Their best friend who has never been to your home. Their nemesis. Their mentors. Their fears, ambitions, dreams, and core values. You need to know if you can trust them. And if they trust you. You need to have a complete mental database on who they are and what makes them tick.

Put another way, you need to know stuff about them that they don't know that you know. Why? Because you never know when this information will come in handy.

Some examples may help:

Let's say your son gets cut from the sophomore baseball team. It's important to know that peanut-butter parfait is his favorite flavor of ice cream.

If your daughter has her heart broken by a boneheaded young man who wasn't worthy of her anyway, it's important to know that yellow roses are her favorite flower.

If one of your children gets in trouble at school or their grades begin to slip, one of the first questions to ask yourself is what recent changes have they been going through. A dad who spies on his kid may have that answer.

The reasons to know your children well extend beyond enduring negative situations. Any extra knowledge you acquire about what makes them tick can help give you hero status in their eyes.

If you overhear your son idolizing a friend's new video-game controller, you have the inside track on the perfect birthday present.

If you know that your teenager is meeting up with friends at the Friday football game, you can proactively make your home a postgame destination by stoking your backyard fire pit and picking up some graham crackers, marshmallows, and Hershey bars.

If a family trip takes you through Ohio, information gathered while spying on your kids will help you decide whether you should schedule a stop in Canton to the see the Football Hall of Fame or Cleveland to tour the Rock and Roll Hall of Fame. On the surface, you may think your son is a huge football fan. After all, he seems to enjoy his time at Cornhusker or Packer games with you. The truth may be that his first love is Coldplay or U2 or The Fray. Knowing this fact is the difference between being a typical dad and being an indisputable hero. At the very least, don't be the dad who drags his kids to the Trapshooting Hall of Fame in Vandalia or the Accounting Hall of Fame in Columbus. (Unless that's who they are and that's what fascinates them.)

Knowing your children's secret worlds can help you appreciate them as individuals, guide them in their area of strength, create opportunities, and keep them out of trouble. The goal is for your kids to pause occasionally and think, *My dad gets it. He understands who I am.* They'll never say that kind of thing out loud of course, but once you establish yourself as a trustworthy insider, you may find that your father-child connections are deeper and conversations are more meaningful. Especially as they plow deeper into those teenage years.

So, how do you spy on your kids without invading their privacy? Diaries and dresser drawers are off limits. Searching book bags and computer histories is not acceptable. Using Jack Bauer techniques to interrogate their friends is probably a bad idea. But here's what you can do:

Offer to drive car pools. It's amazing what you can hear and overhear when you're driving a car full of kids from house to school to practice to lessons to church to the mall and back. You don't have to initiate conversation. It's actually better if they forget you're there. Don't turn on talk radio unless it's a decoy. Once in a while, you can ask whoever is riding shotgun to find a good station. But for the most part, just sit back, sneak an occasional peek in the rearview mirror, and get a glimpse of a little slice of their life.

Network with other parents. We have a saying in our house: "Our spies are everywhere." It sounds like a joke, but it's not. We know hundreds of parents and they know our kids. Sure, sometimes it seems like our kids are overscheduled and involved in way too many group activities, but all those kids in all those events have parents. Those parents are an extra set of eyes and ears. I'm not saying that "it takes a village to raise a child." Raising our children is a job for which my wife and I take full responsibility, but it's still a blessing to have other parents in the neighborhood, on the sidelines, in the auditorium, and just living life in our hometown who care about my kids. Having my kids on the radar screen of other parents is not intimidating. Just the opposite. It's a comfort for Rita and me—and our kids.

Be tech-savvy. Whether it's MySpace, Facebook, or the latest variation of social interactive Web sites, you need to set yourself up with primary or second-generation access. You don't have to have multiple accounts yourself, but stay connected with parents and other individuals who are in the know and in the loop. Expect that sometime, someplace, your teenager is going to be at a gathering where something dangerous or illegal is going down. The good news (and the bad news) is that there's a tattletale in every crowd and the dirt will show up on Facebook. Don't overreact. Don't accuse. Your child may be totally innocent, but because it's public knowledge, you have the right and responsibility to get the facts.

Stand in the middle of their bedroom. When the house is empty, walk in to their room and just observe. Don't rifle through their things. Maybe don't even touch anything at all. But do make note of the environment they have created intentionally or quite by accident. Do a 180° turn. Imagine what their life is like. Remember your fears and fantasies when you were their age. Get in their heads. Yes, you can pull a book off a shelf or pick up a CD. It's permissible to read any poster, catalog, or paper that's in plain sight, but not much more than that. Spend two minutes once a month in their world, and then leave without a trace.

Absorb what they absorb. Read some of the stuff they read. Watch some of the stuff they watch. Listen to some of the stuff they listen to. Play some of the games they play. You may fall asleep at the formulaic animated features. You may roll your eyes at the simplistic teen-angst comedies. You may be disturbed at suggestive music lyrics or the graphic nature of some popular movies or television shows. You may get angry at some of the worldview opinions expressed in the stuff they read. As you immerse yourself in their culture, you'll know more about your kids. A word of caution here: Don't automatically assume your kids endorse or mimic everything they watch, read, or hear. As they sample culture, like you, they're going to consider, judge, and accept or reject what's offered.

To any young people reading this—including my own kids—please understand this spying business is a good thing. Every dad I know wants to do his very best to protect and provide for his children. This is part of that. If and when we go too far, please let us know. Truly, we only want what's best for you.

Finally, if your spying turns up evidence that your son or daughter is endangering their life, then all ironclad rules of privacy and normal parental protocol are off. Your child's survival is more important than their "trust." As a matter of fact, if they're hitting bottom and making life-threatening decisions, they "trust" you to intervene. Also, because you're part of the parenting network, other families are counting on you to do the same for them.

--- **Takeaway** ---

Enter your children's world. Be intentional about knowing more about who they are and what influences their lives.

> *"Outings are so much more fun when we can*
> *savor them through the children's eyes."*
> —LAWANA BLACKWELL

11

Kids Need Their Dad...

Two Words: *Wallet Photos*

M ost of us carry too much stuff in our wallets. Too many credit cards. Too many preferred-guest cards. Too many gift, ID, reward, and punch cards. Our wallets bulge with dog-eared business cards, movie stubs, restaurant receipts, and faded scraps of paper on which we scribbled a name and a phone number but can't remember who they are or why it was important enough to save. If this doesn't describe your wallet, then I'm a little jealous. On occasion my wife even refers to my billfold as a "George Costanza wallet." That's a reference to an old episode of *Seinfeld* in which George's wallet is so overstuffed that it explodes on the street in a shower of receipts and confetti.

When it comes to wallets, the thinner the better. Except for one key element. A few well-chosen, recent family photos.

When I bring this topic up at men's events, I'll stop and give the audience two minutes to pull out their wallets and share their photos with the guys sitting nearby. The response has become predictable.

Half the guys have no photos at all (or maybe no wallet). A third have ancient school photos of some or all of their kids. A very small percentage have recent photos of each member of their family—including their wife. Fathers who recently went through a birth, family wedding, or graduation do a little better. Overall, dads fall way short in this department.

Admittedly, in recent years a new social phenomenon has brought a shift to this fathers-without-photos situation. Younger dads and tech-savvy dads may very well carry dozens or even hundreds of photos in their pockets courtesy of their iPods, iPhones, Blackberries, or other digital storage device.

This is an encouraging trend. Personally, I'm more of a photos-in-the-wallet kind of guy. But I certainly appreciate the convenience and versatility of a PDA or camera phone, and how those devices may usher in a new era of fathers showing off photos of their kids.

When a dad carries photos of his family, three things happen.

One, *he thinks about his children more.* That's a good thing. Every time he pulls out his billfold, he's holding a piece of his family, a piece of his heart.

Two, *his kids feel the connection.* As I've said, kids are smarter than we think they are. They know what's in your wallet. They know the photo you're carrying (and they probably hate the way they look).

Three, *it's a hedge of protection for your marriage.* Every time you pull out your wallet or PDA to show pics of your family, you are telling the world that you place a high value on your relationship with your wife and kids. You're off limits to flirting. You're working to support a cause greater than yourself. You're more likely to head straight home after work. On road trips, you're more likely to go souvenir shopping and catch an earlier flight home than hit the strip clubs and go barhopping all night long. Your expense account might even reflect your more sensible lifestyle. It shouldn't be a surprise that management prefers to give promotions and increased responsibility to guys like that.

Dad, take your kids everywhere you go. Whether they're in a fat wallet or a slim iPhone, don't leave home without them. And hey, if you see me at an airport, convention, or men's event, stop and ask me about my kids. I'll show you mine if you show me yours.

Takeaway

Update your family wallet photos. Get a new plastic insert for your wallet if you have to. Download some new photos or videos on your iPod or Blackberry. Show them off this week.

"What's in your wallet?"
TV COMMERCIALS, CAPITAL ONE

#12

Kids Need Their Dad...

To Answer Their Questions with Questions

Kids ask questions. That's what they do. That's one of the best parts of being a kid. If someone they trust is nearby, they might even ask those questions buzzing through their little heads right out loud. If things go well, they keep asking tougher and tougher questions the rest of their life. The good news, Dad, is that when they're young you know most of the answers. (A few years later, you may have to do a little research, which isn't so bad either.)

How you respond to that first flurry of curiosity will have a long-term impact. If you're not careful, you can squash the itch for knowledge without knowing it. When they ask a question you can ignore it, roll your eyes at it, shoo it away, or deflect it to your child's mom. Problem solved, right? But also opportunity lost. Maybe forever.

Here's an example:

"Dad, at night when there are no stars, where do they go?"

Now you may not have even considered that concept since you were four years old, but with two seconds of thought your adult mind will come up with the answer. One option would be tell your curious child the answer:

"They are hidden by the clouds."

Good answer, Dad. You are indeed smarter than a second-grader. But there's a much better option. Do what Jesus did. Answer a question with a question.

In Matthew, chapter 22, the Pharisees asked Jesus, "Is it right to pay

taxes to Caesar or not?" Jesus held up a denarius and replied, "Whose like-
ness and title is on this coin?"

In Luke 10, an expert in the laws asks, "Teacher, what should I do to
inherit eternal life?" Jesus replied, "What does the law of Moses say? How
do you read it?"

In Mark 8, his disciples exclaimed, "How are we supposed to find enough
food to feed them out here in the wilderness?" Jesus asked, "How much
bread do you have?"

There's a wonderful old proverb that says, "Give a man a fish and he eats
for a day, but teach a man to fish and he eats for a lifetime." We need to
teach our children to think for themselves, to consider all sides of a question, to launch into all the possible answers, both abstract and concrete. By
answering a question with a question, you force the little gears in their minds
to spin. You are teaching them to fish for the very best answer. Let's face it,
you will not always be there with quick and accurate solutions and guidance.
The road ahead for your youngster is paved with many tough questions. If
they practice answering questions with you by their side, then you'll still be
there figuratively, even when you're not there literally.

Which brings us back to the proper answer for that question about a
starless night. You need to respond with something like, "Where do you
think they are?" If they hesitate, you can prompt them with additional questions. "Are the stars still there?" "How can something be there, and you not
see it?" "Are your eyes open?" "Is there something in the way?" "What are
stars anyway?" "What if a star was a lot closer? What would it look like?"
"Could the sun be a star?"

You see where this is going, right? Then, of course, you can always insert
a silly question. "What if all the stars just decided to play hide and seek?"
"What if it's God's birthday and he blew out all the stars because he thought
they were candles?"

As they get older, your questions can dig deeper intellectually and spiritually. "Where do the stars go during the day?" "What's more important—
the moon or the stars?" "If you were lost, could you use the stars to help you
get home?" "How did the stars get there in the first place?"

In the give and take of Q & A, you will discover all kinds of teachable
moments. You can even feel free to throw in a little Scripture once in a
while. "You know, in Psalms it says God counts all the stars and calls them
all by name."

Dad, any time you can extend a short question into a long conversation with your kid, do it. When they're a little bit older, they may not have as much time to talk and you'll miss those conversations. Make sure they miss them too.

Takeaway

Kids are smarter than you think. Even more than asking questions, they love to answer questions. They want to show their dad how smart they are.

"When we have arrived at the question, the answer is already near."
—Ralph Waldo Emerson (1803–1882)

13

Kids Need Their Dad...

To Buy Peeps the First Day They Hit the Shelves

My bride Rita loves Peeps, those frighteningly addictive marshmallow-covered-with-flavored-sugar bunnies and chicks that come out every Easter. She loves them and is quick to point out that they are low in calories and are fat-free. (For the record: Each Peep has 28 calories, one gram of protein and, yes, zero fat.)

Well, Rita never has to buy Peeps.

Somewhere along the way, it became a tradition for the first person in the family who notices that Peeps have arrived in the local drugstore to buy a package for Rita. It has almost become a contest. In the weeks leading up to Easter, Peeps arrive via courier, U.S. Postal Service, mysterious packages left on the front porch, or hand delivery. Last spring, my sons Alec and Max, both working adults, showed up with at least six packages of Peeps. One of every color available.

Here's the point. I started this tradition. But I no longer buy Peeps. I don't have to. Which is fine with me because, frankly, I don't even like Peeps. I do, however, like the tradition. It's one more inside joke, one more time-honored part of family folklore that unites and defines us. Best of all, it's a family-building tradition I don't even have to think about anymore. It has a life of its own. If I get hit by a truck next winter, friends and family members would still buy Peeps for Rita in the spring. That's a good thing. (Not the truck, the tradition.)

Like so much of the wisdom in this book, the Payleitner family Peeps tradition was totally serendipitous. As a dad, if you stick around long enough to be part of the ebb and flow of life, then emotionally satisfying, healthy family traditions will inevitably develop. These are not huge expensive rituals that require extensive planning and scheduling. (Not to say that extravagant traditions are unimportant. Every year you probably should budget hundreds of dollars and clear your calendar for Thanksgiving feasts, a day at Six Flags, an outing to Wrigley Field or Fenway Park, a week at the lake, a shopping excursion to the American Girl store, and so on.)

But the quirky little traditions unique to your family are just as important. Maybe more important. Especially if they come with triggers that don't require any preparation.

Examples? The first nice weekend of summer could trigger a family bike ride. The first snowfall of the year that has "good packing" could trigger a family snowball fight. When the local community college or high school presents their annual musical, pull the trigger and go to the Sunday matinee. When Shamrock Shakes come out at McDonald's, that could trigger a family dessert run. When the church across town holds their "live Nativity scene," don't miss it. When the zoo announces a new baby giraffe or lion cub, it goes without saying that your family will be one of the first in line to see the little cutie.

As hard as you try, I'm not sure you can orchestrate these kinds of family traditions. They just happen. So be warned. To a kid, if you do something just twice, they expect it to become a regular, time-honored, unwritten law set in stone. As my daughter, Rae Anne, said years ago when insisting we stop for cones at an ice cream store near the bike trail, "We have to stop here. It's a tradition!" And you know what? She was right.

Takeaway

Pause to consider the small time-honored traditions unique to your family. Especially things you don't plan, but are triggered by occasional or annual events. There's probably one coming up in the next couple weeks. Don't miss it.

"What an enormous magnifier is tradition! How a thing grows in the human memory and in the human imagination, when love, worship, and all that lies in the human heart, is there to encourage it."
—Thomas Carlyle (1795–1881)

Kids Need Their Dad...

To Understand the Ebb and Flow of Traditions

For 22 years, we had an annual Easter egg hunt. At 10 a.m. on the day before Easter. It grew from one cousin and a few neighbors to more than 50 kids from 20 families. At its peak, we were filling more than 750 plastic eggs with jelly beans, stickers, and other goodies. It was part entertainment, part outreach. When the time came, I would do an ever-so-short devotional reminding the kids (and their assembled parents) about the real truth of Easter, say a short prayer, and give the egg-hunting rules. Then the scramble was on.

In general, I believe that three-day period from Good Friday to Resurrection Sunday should remain solemn and contemplative, but a lot of good came out of the fun and festivities of that annual tradition. Families got together. The source of Grace was articulated. We extended invitations to Easter services the next day. Memories were made.

Over the years, as the older kids got older, they would transition from egg-finders to egg-hiders. Finally, when our youngest, Rae Anne, turned nine, we decided to put the tradition on hold until grandkids came along. (We're still waiting.) We thought about keeping it going for the other families who looked forward to it every year, but all their kids were getting older as well. It was difficult, but for now the laundry basket of plastic eggs waits in the basement for the next generation.

The good news is that a new Payleitner family Easter tradition has taken its place. Sort of. This new tradition is not on Saturday morning. It's after

51

service and brunch on Easter Sunday and does not include dozens of toddlers and school-age kids. It's just for our own family. It's stickball. In the driveway. With a broom handle and Wiffle balls. The strike zone is an old lawn chair leaned up against the garage door. The teams are Alec and Isaac versus Max and Randy. The competitors wear silly shorts, old jerseys, and jaunty baseball caps. The spectators who sit on the parkway grass and enjoy the curve balls, home runs, and diving catches include Rita, Jay, and Rae Anne (who, ironically, may be the best athlete of all my kids). The most recent addition to the cheering section is our delightful daughter-in-law, Rachel, who fits right in.

So after years of meticulous and labor-intensive planning and yard preparation for Easter weekend, this new tradition kind of just happens without any parental involvement. My bride and I just sit back and enjoy. It's kind of nice.

Holding tightly to traditions in the moment sets the stage for holding them loosely enough to know when to let them go. Kids get older. Homes are bought and sold. Family members pass on. New family members bring their own traditions. Sometimes tragedy leads to change. Often, it's just time and circumstance.

For 30 years, until 1978, three generations of Payleitners went to the same big cottage on Pine Lake in Wisconsin for a week each summer. But it just didn't make sense after Grandpa died.

For 20 years, we dragged our kids to a department store for photos with Santa Claus. The photo album begins with just Alec in 1980, but a new sibling enters in '83, '86, '88, and '93. For some reason, Alec just didn't want to sit on Santa's lap after he turned 21 and that's where the photo album ends.

For the 12 years we lived on Weber Road, a visit to just one or two bedrooms would enable me to tuck in all my kids, read bedtime stories, and have some great end-of-day conversations. When we moved to Tyler Road, suddenly the kids were sleeping in four different rooms and the enchanting nighttime ritual faded away. That loss still makes me sad. (You may want to remember that, Dad, when you consider moving to a bigger house or when a child says, "I want my own room.")

Still, some traditions have remarkable staying power.

For more than 50 years, every June still finds a bunch of us sitting on the curb at the two-hour long Swedish Days Parade in Geneva, Illinois. Our attendance fluctuates between 10 and 25 people depending on schedule conflicts brought on by softball, baseball, volleyball, graduation parties, and work. The responsibility for planning and providing postparade activities has changed several times over the decades, but still the day remains a high priority for our entire extended family.

That ability to flex and go with the flow may be the secret to traditions that last through multiple generations. Sometimes, parade routes change or the lake house gets sold. Sometimes, bigger and better options pull key family members away—like new babies, military service, mission trips, book tours, and once-in-a-lifetime travel opportunities.

Challenges like death, divorce, extended illness, long-distance moves, and family squabbles can take their toll on the most cherished family traditions. On the other hand, reviving or tweaking those traditions may help reunite your family. Making sure your crew gets together on a regular basis is one of the most important things a dad can do.

Takeaway

Ultimately, family traditions should bring anticipation and joy. Not drudgery or burden. When the time comes, it's okay to let go without guilt or remorse. Sometimes, the more loosely you hold on to something, the better it can evolve into something new and even more meaningful. Letting others take ownership can be a blessing for all.

> *"Civilization is impossible without traditions, and progress impossible without the destruction of those traditions. The difficulty, and it is an immense difficulty, is to find a proper equilibrium between stability and variability."*
> —GUSTAVE LE BON (1841–1931)

15

Kids Need Their Dad...

To Ignore (or Even Applaud) the Dents on the Garage Door

Much to the amusement of the neighbors in our cul-de-sac, the front yard of our two-story brick-and-aluminum-sided suburban home has seen quite an array of activity over the years.

In addition to stickball on Easter Sunday afternoon (and other days), our driveway has been the site of a pig roast, a sidewalk chalk art gallery, intense four-square contests, amateur auto body shop repair, unicycle riding, tandem bike maintenance, science experiments including the old Mentos in the Diet Coke trick, home-run derby, homecoming pep-rally practices, skateboard/bike skiing, and slam-dunk contests. One year, to celebrate their high-school graduation, we crafted an 8-foot by 12-foot mosaic of Isaac and his cousin Stephanie made entirely out of 3-inch x 3-inch Post-It Notes and posted it on our garage door.

Speaking of garage doors, I finally replaced ours about five years ago. It cost me $1200 and made all the difference in the world when you pulled up to our home. That new garage door was crisp, clean, and flawless—for about a month. I had selected a heavy-duty grade so that the Wiffle balls wouldn't leave a dent. But once in a while on the back swing, the stickball bat will strike the garage door with enough force to leave a noticeable crease in the surface. (I think Jacob Grossman may have been the initial culprit, but I'm not pointing any fingers.)

How did I, as a father, react to those fresh dents in my fresh garage door? Actually, I did pretty well. My mind quickly calculated the value of the events that had taken place that afternoon in my very own driveway, and I knew I had come out way ahead. My teenage sons and some of their life-long friends had chosen to hang out in my front yard. No beer cans in sight. No police squad cars pulling up with bad news. No video games crashing and slashing in a dark basement. These young men were playing the time-honored game of stickball. What kind of investment does that require? Broom handle: $3. Wiffle balls: $6. A garage door with stickball bruises: priceless. (Marked down from $1200.)

A home is to be lived in. If you have kids and tend to stress out every time a floor gets scuffed, a table gets scratched, or a door gets dented, your home is not going to be a place where young people want to hang out. In our community, there's a tradition among high-school students that when you enter a house you kick off your shoes at the front door. I want to tell the kids not to worry about our carpets, but I'm glad for the show of respect. I'm also amused at the dozens of sneakers, boots, sandals, Crocs, and Birken-stocks, which create quite a pile in our foyer. Make your home a place that kids feel comfortable, and you'll always know where your own kids are and who they're with.

There's a great story told by Harmon Killebrew, the All-Star power hit-ter for the Minnesota Twins. He once said, "My father used to play with my brother and me in the yard. Mother would come out and say, 'You're tearing up the grass.' 'We're not raising grass,' Dad would reply. 'We're rais-ing boys.'"

Takeaway

You've heard it before, but it's worth repeating. Your kids grow up so fast. They'll be gone before you know it. After that, you'll have plenty of time to re-sod, re-paint, re-screen, re-carpet, and relax.

"The most important things in your home are people."
—BARBARA JOHNSON (1841–1931)

16

Kids Need Their Dad...

To Avoid the Clichés

Did you hear these growing up? Some of the following expressions may sound vaguely familiar. My fear, of course, is that I use them way too often and my kids see right through every word. There may be great truths hidden in these classic parenting clichés, but that doesn't mean we can toss them around without any foresight or supporting evidence.

You might want to be especially aware of the ones you heard in your youth and be even more aware of the ones you've heard from your mouth.

"Because I said so."

"Don't put that in your mouth; you don't know where it's been."

"What will the neighbors think?"

"Always wear clean underwear in case you get in a car accident."

"If your brother jumped off a bridge, would you?"

"Don't use that tone with me."

"Look at me when I'm talking to you."

"If you break your leg, don't come running to me."

"Don't cross your eyes, they'll stay that way."

"Stop crying or I'll give you something to cry about."

"Money doesn't grow on trees."

"Don't run with scissors."

"Were you born in a barn?"

"It's all fun and games until someone gets hurt."

"Do you think your socks are going to pick themselves up?"

"What are you waiting for, an engraved invitation?"

"Pretty is as pretty does!"

"Two wrongs do not make a right."

"You're the oldest. You should know better."

"Someone is going to end up crying."

"What did I just get finished telling you?"

"Don't ever let me catch you doing that again."

"I didn't ask who put it there, I said, 'Pick it up!'"

"Pick that up before somebody trips on it and breaks their neck!"

"You must be confusing me with the maid we don't have."

"Put that down! You don't know where it's been!"

"If I want your opinion I'll ask for it!"

"There's enough dirt in those ears to grow potatoes!"

"You just ate an hour ago!"

"If you're bored, I can always find something for you to do."

"Life isn't supposed to be fair."

"Don't make me stop this car!"

"I paid good money for that."

Amused? Convicted? If expressions like these come out of your mouth too easily, you may be guilty of lazy fathering.

Dad, when you're with your kids, do you often take the easy way out? When you babysit the toddlers, do you plop them in front of the TV? Do you insist that volunteering at school is for moms only? Rather than thinking through options and repercussions, do you find yourself using this old cliché—"It's fine with me, but go ask your mother"? Do you hustle home from work for elementary-school band concerts or do you feel that squeaky clarinets are a valid excuse for working late? Is it just easier for you to tackle a home improvement project by yourself, or do you get your child involved and make it a teachable moment? With your teenage daughter, if you give her a credit card and keys to the car, she'll be out of your hair for at least four hours. Is that really what you want? When it comes to their spiritual development, do you believe it's enough to drop the kids off at Sunday school and youth group?

At this point, I could offer another parenting cliché: "Parenting is hard work." But you know something…really, it's not. Being the kind of dad you want to be does require creativity, energy, persistence, and lots and lots of time. It might leave you exhausted and penniless. But without a doubt, the reward for your investment comes back a hundredfold.

Got it? "Now don't make me repeat myself!"

Takeaway

Every day presents a new opportunity to be the dad. If you missed it yesterday, make sure you grab onto it today.

> *"Having a family is like having a bowling*
> *alley installed in your brain."*
>
> —MARTIN MULL

#17

Kids Need Their Dad...

To Get Right with *His* Dad

This is a no-brainer for some of you guys reading this. You have a great connection with your father, the lines of communication are open, you get together several times a year (or more), the grandkids love going to see gramps (or whatever name they call him), and you have a genuine need and desire to spend time with him. It's a mutually rewarding relationship. You turn to him for advice. He asks your opinion. With satisfaction, he sees himself in you and your family. Memories are shared. Memories are still being made. The fathering legacy is a joy to pass on to your children, especially your sons.

If that describes the relationship between you and your father, count your blessings and never take for granted the benefits of family love and loyalty through the generations. You're living the truth and the promise of the fifth commandment. "Honor your father and mother. Then you will live a long, full life in the land the LORD your God is giving you" (Exodus 20:12 NLT). In Ephesians 6:2, Paul points out that this is the only one of the Ten Commandments that comes with a promise. Clearly, honoring the past generation makes life a whole lot easier for the next.

On the other hand, I am well aware that for a lot of guys any kind of close relationship with your father sounds way too good to be true. You may be one of those men suffering from decades of painful baggage and bad blood. Over the years, you and your father may have built a wall that seems unlikely ever to come down.

This chapter is way too short and this author is way too unqualified to walk most of you through a process of father-son reconciliation. But this chapter tucked into the middle of a book for dads may be able to do one thing. It can help you decide whether or not you should pursue that reconciliation...and how to begin.

Ask yourself a few key questions. Was your father abusive? Did he abandon you? Was there criminal or immoral behavior? Not to dig up old wounds, but you may be carrying some emotional scars that require healing. Consider opening your heart to a trusted friend, loving wife, wise pastor, or professional counselor. Even if you never speak to your father again, you may be able to find closure or a sense of peace.

On the other hand, some of you need to actually *talk* to your dad. If he's alive, there's still time. Every situation is different, and the last thing I want to do is oversimplify what you have experienced. But consider this: Think for a moment about how much you love your children. You would give your life for them, right? Is it possible that your father—wherever he is and whatever he has done—had that same feeling for you? Or still does?

What would happen if you picked up the phone this very day and said, "I regret what has happened between us. Can we make things right?" Would he slam down the phone? Would he weep with joy?

I apologize if these few paragraphs have left you weak with regret or raging with anger. But if just a handful of men reunite or reconnect with their older counterpart, then the effort has been worth it. Don't you agree?

For those of you who have lost your father through death or distance, the process of forgiving your father or moving beyond the pain is still within your reach. Just about every professional psychologist would encourage you not to bury it. There's no shame in admitting the need to find peace with the memory of your father.

Which brings us full circle to your relationship with your own children. Much of what you know about fathering you learned (or didn't learn) from your own father. Other men may have come into your life, but there's undoubtedly one man you have put on that fathering pedestal and his legacy is what you carry for better or worse. Your mandate is to take the best and chuck the rest.

If he taught you some valuable skills, habits, or lessons, hang on to them tightly. If he had little or nothing to give, then let it go. If there's dysfunction, choose to break the chain. If there's love and nurturance, you've been given the privilege of passing it on to the next generation and beyond.

Takeaway

Maybe…call your dad. Thank him. Forgive him. Ask his forgiveness. Ask for his blessing. Visit his gravesite. Tell your kids something good about him.

> *"Our children give us the opportunity to become*
> *the parents we always wished we'd had."*
> —LOUISE HART

18

Kids Need Their Dad...

To Rent a Dolphin for an Hour

The Payleitner family has always traveled on a budget. With five kids, any vacation destination that has a "cost per child" adds up pretty quickly. A day at a theme park can easily cost more than $100 per person per day. Throw in food and lodging and it adds up even faster. That's why Rita and I would always think long and hard before taking our crew on any major excursion.

So how could I justify spending $70 per kid (that's $350) on one hour of entertainment? I'm still not sure how it happened. But it was worth every nickel.

Here was the circumstance. It was the end of February 2003. After an exhausting but successful high-school wrestling season for Max and Isaac, we were inspired to try and squeeze in a much-needed break before the baseball season began. Rae Anne was almost ten. Could the five of us find some sunshine for an extra long weekend? We had never been to the Florida Keys, airfare was cheap, and I had just finished a freelance project that would cover the cost.

With less than two weeks before departure, I began charting a detailed itinerary. (My kids and wife mock me because I tend to go, go, go on vacations rather than relax, relax, relax. But it's about cramming in as many memories as possible, right?)

As we envisioned our time together, Rita and I realized we would definitely miss our older sons, but clearly there was no way they could get away. Randy had a full load of classes at the University of Illinois and Alec was working full-time in Chicago. Still, we let them both know they were invited.

Amazingly, both boys cleared their schedules, and suddenly the seven Pay-leitners were spending four days together in Key Largo, Marathon, and Key West, Florida.

Now about that dolphin. Typically, when presented with a menu of options, I go with the middle choice. The medium Slurpee. The mid-priced photo package. The polyester/wool-blend suit. Seats in the mezzanine, rather than balcony or box seats. As I researched "things to do in the Keys," I came across several attractions featuring a chance to interact with dolphins. You could watch them perform from a distance. You could lean into the pool and actually pet them. Or, you could swim with them. My initial instinct was "pet the dolphins." What a great experience that would be. Then, for some unexpected reason, I went for it all. I dialed the phone, pulled out my credit card, and we were booked.

Over those few days in south Florida, my family walked the edge of the Everglades, went snorkeling off a pontoon boat, climbed a lighthouse, and lay on the beach. We had pizza in the hotel room one night and had a couple nice family dinners out. (Alec even picked up the tab one evening.) But we all agree the highlight was swimming with the dolphin. Our own dolphin.

At the aquatic center, as they divided us into groups, we requested to be kept together. When they realized that my five kids were all in one family, they assigned us one trainer and one dolphin for the entire hour. Alec, Randy, Max, Isaac, and Rae Anne all had three turns with "Stormy." They hugged and kissed her, they zipped alongside her on a dorsal tow, and they each got a high speed "foot push" around the inlet. Rita and I just watched, cheered, and videotaped. It was a total blast.

Of course, vacations end and life goes on. But the memory remains. That surprising hour we spent together has made our family ever-so-much stronger.

The point is that sometimes—not always—but sometimes, a dad needs to bite the bullet and invest in the best (that is, most expensive) option for that particular moment on behalf of his family. Don't risk your retirement funds or sacrifice any savings for the kids' college education, but once in a while the best decision is to splurge.

Dad, can you imagine these words coming out of your mouth? "Banana splits for everyone." "Honey, why don't you get all three pairs." "Maybe it's time for that big-screen TV." "Oh by the way, Sunday afternoon we're all going on a hot-air-balloon ride!" Once in a while that's the right choice to make.

Finally, it's worth noting that a moment of unbridled generosity is even more surprising if you've been extra miserly in recent months. So make it a regular habit to model good stewardship. Don't apologize for saying "no" to your kids when they ask for something. Despite what other families do, kids don't always need the newest and shiniest. Truthfully, being frugal is almost always the best choice.

But I totally recommend swimming with the dolphins.

Takeaway

If you've been pinching pennies for quite a while, at the right time and place, splurge on something wonderful and worthwhile. On the other hand, if your kids always experience the biggest and the best, introduce them to the concept of "less is more."

> *"Do not store up for yourselves treasures on earth, where moth and rust destroy, and where thieves break in and steal. But store up for yourselves treasures in heaven, where moth and rust do not destroy, and where thieves do not break in and steal. For where your treasure is, there your heart will be also."*
>
> —Matthew 6:19-21

#19

Kids Need Their Dad...

To Acknowledge the Absurdity of Participation Trophies

I t never fails. On the first day of practice of far too many organized youth sports teams, the well-meaning coach stands in front of his eager athletes and parents and says, "The most important thing is to have fun."

And I just want to gag.

Hold on, don't flip out. Just to be clear: I am a fun guy. Put me in front of a group of third-graders and I am the funnest guy you know. Fun is my middle name.

But if the coach really thinks the most important thing is "to have fun," he has already failed. He has failed to take advantage of a momentous opportunity to make a lifelong positive impact on these children, whether they're girls, boys, or both. You might even say that coach has failed his community, because years from now when the varsity coaches are looking for point guards, shortstops, hurdlers, and sweepers, those athletes will not be equipped to get the job done for their high-school team. Or beyond. Conference trophies will go to another school. Individual college scholarships will not be awarded. Potential Olympic champions will remain undiscovered.

Let me tell you the most important thing for a coach to do with a rag-tag group of raw recruits who are about to dedicate an entire season of their lives to his coaching philosophy. No, I'm not going to say, "Winning is everything." (Yes, it is fun to win, but that's actually pretty far down on the list of importance.)

What every coach needs to do is commit to providing every member of his team with at least one authentic moment of success on the playing field sometime during the season.

Let me say it another way. Beginning with five-year-old soccer players, six-year-old T-ball players, or nine-year-old flag football players, the job of a head coach is to orchestrate moments of unmistakable accomplishment, thereby demonstrating the value of hard work and perseverance and creating memories of earned achievement.

Said still another way: Make sure each kid does something he'll remember with a smile.

It's not easy. But Coach, please take this to heart. Clearly, each boy or girl brings a different level of experience, knowledge, God-given ability, and parental involvement. Still, each athlete (or nonathlete) has been placed on your team so that they can take their game to the next level.

Examples? For the first time ever, Becca makes contact with the ball and runs hard to first. For the first time, Todd sets his feet, stays low, and holds his block. Carlos gets his first takedown, the one you drilled all week. Superstar ball hog Ryan finally passes to the open man for an assist. Truly, these are breakthrough moments—moments to remember.

Did you win every game? Did you take the league championship? It doesn't matter. Did each of these kids do something they had never done before? You bet they did, and Coach, it's your job to notice. In the huddle after each game, point out those heroes by name: "John, the way you charged that bunt was exactly right." "Lisa, you were seeing the whole field today. Your pass to Beth was outstanding." "Rachel, your free throws in the third quarter changed the momentum of the entire game." John, Lisa, and Rachel may never play another season of baseball, soccer, or basketball, but your words will stay with them for the rest of their lives. That feeling of taking their game to the next level will serve them well as they pursue excellence in academia, business, parenting, the creative arts, and so on.

By the end of the season, you'll want to make sure everyone has been singled out for one or two moments of personal accomplishment. Not fake moments, because kids can smell baloney a mile away. You need to find or orchestrate authentic moments of success for every single individual on the squad. For some players, that can be quite a challenge. If Brian can barely pick up a grounder and couldn't possibly throw across the infield, then put him at second and make sure your best player is at first to scoop up Brian's terrible throw. After about four innings, when he finally does record that 4-3 put-out, you've done a great thing for Brian and his parents.

For a child, accomplishing something they have never done before and gaining a sincere compliment from a coach they respect is the exact opposite of "participation trophies." If you're in the trophy-making business, I'm sorry. But somewhere around 1980 (or maybe earlier) a well-intentioned coach got the idea that kids should get a piece of glistening hardware just for showing up. Yikes.

Kids know the difference between a $20 trophy awarded merely for showing up and a 75-cent ribbon earned for second place in the potato-sack race. Which do you think they would rather have? (If you believe your child would say, "Gimme the trophy," just wait a few years. They'll soon appreciate the value of earned accolades.)

To all those coaches that put the highest priority on having fun, I have one thing to say. You don't have a clue what fun is.

In the world of athletics, fun is setting your sights on a goal and reaching it. Fun is accomplishing something you never thought possible. Fun is breaking an eight-game losing streak. Fun is watching a hardworking teammate break a school record. Fun is losing in double overtime to a team that crushed you by a wide margin earlier in the season. To be sure, fun is the bus ride home with your sweaty teammates knowing that victory came only because of the extra effort each one of you put in to prepare for that game.

Will every moment of every practice be fun? I hope not. Will each athlete in your charge look forward to stretching themselves and working toward new goals and achieving recognition for authentic accomplishment? That's the idea. And that's a blast.

For some athletes, their time on your team may help launch them to college scholarships and a career of scrapbooks filled with clippings and awards. It's okay for you to take a small measure of pride in their achievement.

For other members of your team, you might be the last coach they ever have, because next season they choose to move on to use other gifts in non-athletic endeavors. But they'll always remember the coach who gave them a little taste of true personal victory.

Takeaway

Young people want to be challenged. When they know that effort is noticed and rewarded, they will give 110 percent. They don't want false praise or accolades for just showing up. And for heaven's sake, let's finally do away with "participation trophies."

> *"It is not the critic who counts,*
> *not the man who points out how the strong man stumbled,*
> *or where the doer of deeds could have done better.*
> *The credit belongs to the man who is actually in the arena;*
> *whose face is marred by the dust and sweat and blood;*
> *who strives valiantly; who errs and comes short again and again;*
> *who knows the great enthusiasms, the great devotions*
> *and spends himself in a worthy cause;*
> *who at the best, in the end, knows the triumph of high achievement,*
> *and who, at worst, if he fails, at least fails while daring greatly;*
> *knowing that his place shall never be among those cold*
> *and timid souls who know neither victory nor defeat."*

—THEODORE ROOSEVELT (1858–1919)

20

Kids Need Their Dad...

To Understand All Three Perspectives in the Story of the Prodigal Son

When's the last time you read the parable of the Prodigal Son? Years? Decades? Ever? Let's take a moment right now to put that story into context and then read it in its entirety.

Back in the first century, Luke was a respected medical doctor and accomplished historian. The first few chapters of the Gospel bearing his name record historically accurate, intimate details surrounding Jesus' birth, baptism, ancestry, and the 40 days he was tempted by the devil in the desert. Luke ends his Gospel recording the events of the last supper, the crucifixion, the resurrection, and Jesus' ascension into heaven. In between, Dr. Luke delivers compelling accounts of Jesus' miracles, prophecies, and teachings.

Jesus' most engaging teaching method was the use of parables. These are fictional allegories he told to make a point. As the greatest teacher of all time, he knew how to weave an engaging yarn...with the purpose of teaching a singular truth. For example, the parable of the Good Samaritan answers the question, "Who is my neighbor?" The parable of the Rich Fool, whose main character kept building bigger and bigger barns, demonstrates that worldly wealth doesn't last. The parable of the Four Soils explains how the seed of God's truth is received or rejected by four different kinds of people.

Luke chapter 15, records Jesus telling the parable of the Prodigal Son. You've likely heard it before, but good stories like this deserve multiple readings and in-depth examination. In Jesus' own words...

A man had two sons. The younger son told his father, "I want my share of your estate now before you die." So his father agreed to divide his wealth between his sons.

A few days later this younger son packed all his belongings and moved to a distant land, and there he wasted all his money in wild living. About the time his money ran out, a great famine swept over the land, and he began to starve. He persuaded a local farmer to hire him, and the man sent him into his fields to feed the pigs. The young man became so hungry that even the pods he was feeding the pigs looked good to him. But no one gave him anything.

When he finally came to his senses, he said to himself, "At home even the hired servants have food enough to spare, and here I am dying of hunger! I will go home to my father and say, 'Father, I have sinned against both heaven and you, and I am no longer worthy of being called your son. Please take me on as a hired servant.'"

So he returned home to his father. And while he was still a long way off, his father saw him coming. Filled with love and compassion, he ran to his son, embraced him, and kissed him. His son said to him, "Father, I have sinned against both heaven and you, and I am no longer worthy of being called your son."

But his father said to the servants, "Quick! Bring the finest robe in the house and put it on him. Get a ring for his finger and sandals for his feet. And kill the calf we have been fattening. We must celebrate with a feast, for this son of mine was dead and has now returned to life. He was lost, but now he is found." So the party began.

Meanwhile, the older son was in the fields working. When he returned home, he heard music and dancing in the house, and he asked one of the servants what was going on. "Your brother is back," he was told, "and your father has killed the fattened calf. We are celebrating because of his safe return."

The older brother was angry and wouldn't go in. His father came out and begged him, but he replied, "All these years I've slaved for you and never once refused to do a single thing you told me to. And in all that time you never gave me even one young goat for a feast with my friends. Yet when this son of yours comes back after squandering your money on prostitutes, you celebrate by killing the fattened calf!"

His father said to him, "Look, dear son, you have always stayed by me, and everything I have is yours. We had to celebrate this happy day. For your brother was dead and has come back to life! He was lost, but now he is found!" (Luke 15:11-32 NLT).

Theologians would say that Jesus was teaching that day about God's unconditional love—that no matter what you've done, he will always celebrate the day when a lost person finally surrenders to grace. That, of course, is the ultimate goal for all of us. But I believe there are at least three additional lessons that can be gleaned from this parable, lessons that all fathers need to understand and file away for future reference. You probably already know what I'm talking about.

The father's response throughout the entire story reminds us to be patient with our children. They are going to disappoint you. They may turn their back on you. They may squander your hard-earned money on "wild living." The example of the prodigal's father models how we need to keep the door open. We may need to wait expectantly. When our prodigal children begin to take a few steps back, run to them. And get ready to party.

Then, put yourself in the shoes of the prodigal son. The world grabbed him and then sucked the life out of him. If you can prevent that from happening to your children, that's tremendous. But some things are out of your control. Even before his money ran out, the young man probably had twinges of regret and remorse. At his lowest point, who did he think of? His dad. We need to make sure our children know they can always, always come home.

Finally, there's the older son. You can't blame him for being jealous. The whole time they were growing up, his twerpy little brother probably got a bigger dose of Mom and Dad's attention. What is this faithful son doing when the homecoming party starts? He's out working in the field! Of course he's ticked! Not surprisingly, the older brother is not quick to forgive and forget. Thankfully, the father doesn't blow him off. Dad knows just what to say. Paraphrasing: "Son, we both know your little brother has been messing up. He deserves a good trip to the woodshed. But you have to admit, you were worried about him too. More than anything, this is a time to celebrate. By the way, I know I haven't thanked you enough for who you are and what you do. You make me proud. If you need something, just ask. What's mine is yours."

Gotta admit, there's some pretty good stuff in those parables.

Takeaway

If a son or daughter turns their back on you, don't turn your back on them.

> *"The LORD is compassionate and gracious, slow to anger,*
> *abounding in love. He will not always accuse, nor will*
> *he harbor his anger forever; he does not treat us as our*
> *sins deserve or repay us according to our iniquities."*
>
> —PSALM 103:8-10

21

Kids Need Their Dad...

To Teach Them the Word *Pneumonoultramicro-scopicsilicovolcanoconiosis*

The *Oxford English* Dictionary says that *pneumonoultramicroscopicsilicovolcanoconiosis* is "a factitious word alleged to mean 'a lung disease caused by the inhalation of very fine silica dust, causing inflammation in the lungs.'" And it's a word your kids would love to know. What makes this word so important? Well, certainly it's a vital piece of information if you happen to be a miner who has spent too much time breathing volcano dust. But other than that, there are not too many practical uses for the word. Except one.

Knowing this word is just cool. Because it's a superlative. This 45-letter word is recognized as the longest word ever to appear in an English-language dictionary. That alone makes it cool. Kids love extremes. The fastest land animal? The biggest dinosaur? The tallest building? You may or may not be surprised at how many third-graders know the answers are cheetah, Argentinosaurus, and the Dubai Tower. Even if they don't know for sure, there's still a fascination with the answers.

Don't think that applies to your kids? Do you think they'd rather watch *Power Rangers*, text their classmates, or walk around a mall? Toss a copy of *The Guinness Book of World Records* on the kitchen table and just watch. Children of all ages will be drawn to it, fascinated by one "-est" after another: the smallest, largest, earliest, longest, shortest, smartest, deepest, strongest, and so on. The more recent issues of *The Guinness Book* don't compare to the 2-inch-thick, fact-filled paperbacks of the 1970s. The new version is more glitz than substance, not so much something you might sit down and read, but rather a coffee table book. Still, the newer large hardcover editions brim with startling photos, odd bits of trivia, and superlatives your kids will discover and want to share...with you. And that's a good thing.

Back to the original premise of this chapter. Should a dad ever sit down and adamantly cram the meaning and pronunciation of *pneumonoultramicroscopicsilicovolcanoconiosis* into the brain of his child? Of course not. But every kid deserves to be given the opportunity. It happened to my oldest son, Alec, sort of accidentally.

Years ago, when Alec was a young teenager, I happened across a little 64-page book by Rick Davis titled *Totally Useless Skills*. For some reason, I bought it and tossed it in my glove compartment. What else do you do with a book like that? You can't bring it in the house because your wife might say, "Why did you buy this book?" (Some things moms just don't get.) Anyway. As promised in the title, the paperback overflowed with a wide range of useless skills, including goofy magic tricks, secrets to crowd-pleasing talents such as juggling and hanging spoons from your nose, and bits of eccentric trivia.

For months, anytime Alec was in the car with me, he would immediately open the glove box, pull out the book, and absorb these skills. Because he's a word guy like his dad, he spent a few extra moments on the page that featured the longest word in the English language. In a short time, he had it memorized and was ready to share it with his chauffeur and the world. I'm not sure how often the word came up in regular conversation, but he was armed with it, just in case.

This particular story culminates years later when Alec appreciatively opens a college graduation present from his mom and me. It's a dictionary he's been coveting for years. *The Compact Edition of the Oxford English Dictionary* weighs more than 15 pounds, but even at that size, the printing is still so tiny (it's reproduced micrographically) that the reader must use the accompanying magnifying glass to decipher any of its entries. (Please don't ask how much we paid for it.) My son, the freshly-graduated English major, lays the magnificent volume on the table before him, pauses, and looks up—what else?—*pneumonoultramicroscopicsilicovolcanoconiosis*.

Please note. I'm not recommending that any dad run out and purchase a 15-pound dictionary or any specific trivia, joke, or record book. The point is that resources are out there. Children's natural curiosity must be fed. Guys, we need to consider ourselves advocates for exploration and eager partners for the journey.

―――――――――――――― **Takeaway** ――――――――――――――

Kids are curious. Use their inquisitive nature as a way to connect with them and as a conduit for helping them discover truth.

> *"Curiosity is one of the most permanent and certain characteristics of a vigorous intellect."*
> —DR. SAMUEL JOHNSON (1709–1784)

#22

Kids Need Their Dad...

To Conquer the Car Seat

Two things about infant car seats.

First, they are a major hassle. With their clasps, straps, button slots, and hinged mechanisms they resemble colorfully padded medieval torture devices. Even worse, for safety reasons, they must be installed in the back seat, which means Mommy or Daddy must reach back and squeeze between bucket seats kicking the dashboard, or sprawl awkwardly across the back caverns of an SUV or minivan to secure the little darlings in place. No matter which seat belt I blindly grab, it's always the wrong one, and even the right one never quite reaches across the entire car seat without a teeth-gritting sequence of tug, retraction, tug, retraction, and so on. It's a good thing newborns have undeveloped language skills. Just a reminder, though—babies do pick up on the tone of your voice, and older siblings do pick up on your choice of word or phrase. All that to say, anytime Dad volunteers to wrestle with the car seat, that scores major points with Mom.

Second, car seats should stay in the car. That's a general rule.

Have you ever been at a gathering when a couple shows up with a newborn in a car seat? That kid is a foot off the ground and a foot from any human contact, and Dad is swinging that car seat. What happens when the baby cries? He swings the car seat faster. When I see that I want to scream, "*Hold* your baby!" Newborns need to be held. They need to feel the touch of your skin. They need to feel the rhythm of Mom or Dad's heartbeat. Think about where they just came from! For the first couple months of life, the more you hold them and gently talk to them, the better. They are learning how to love and be loved. And those are two of the most important skills anyone ever learns.

Studies have shown that all newborns require a certain amount of physical contact every day. If they don't get it, they suffer from a withdrawal condition known as "failure to thrive." Also called "maternal deprivation syndrome," it's a fatal psychosocial condition that is actually quite common in understaffed orphanages around the world. Years ago, I visited several such orphanages in Russia. I will never forget watching a single nurse care for a ward full of infants. With so little human contact, it's hard to imagine those children growing into healthy adults that reach their God-given potential. With maternal deprivation syndrome, babies don't have enough human contact...so they just give up.[8]

I realize there is zero chance that your little bundle of joy is going to die from lack of human contact, but doesn't it make sense that the opposite— *lots* of intimate contact—helps launch them into a life filled with love, wisdom, passion, joy, and laughter?

So leave the car seat in the car. And hold your baby. And Dad, that's not just a Mom's job. You also have the privilege of snuggling, soothing, and kissing that baby who needs so desperately to feel your love.

Takeaway

Hold your baby.

> *"Babies are such a nice way to start people."*
> DON HEROLD (1889–1966)

Kids Need Their Dad...

To Affirm Their
Existence Intellectually

I'm hoping this chapter doesn't sound like psychobabble. If it starts to feel like you need to get out a pair of hip waders, try to keep going, because this is an important concept to more children than you might think. Some of them carry it into adulthood.

Here goes. All kids need to *hear* the words "I love you." You already knew that. All kids need to *feel* love. That also is not a surprise. Things like investing time, keeping promises, hugs, discipline, and provision all help to fill that need. For most kids, hearing and feeling love is usually enough to fill their "love cup."

Still, a percentage of kids need additional intellectual affirmation that they are loved and valued. Sometimes, circumstances beyond your control create an environment in which a child starts to believe, "Maybe I'm not worthy," "Maybe I don't belong," "Maybe I'm damaged or unwanted goods." Babies and children are such an awesome gift that it's hard to imagine such a feeling, but it happens. How a dad responds can help dispel these feelings quite efficiently. A father's few well-chosen words or his taking a firm stand can turn a potential emotional disaster into a minor momentary misunderstanding that has little or no impact.

Consider this scenario. Let's say you've got four kids. Three young adults and one preschooler. The family joke is that junior is an "oops baby." But if junior hears that, it's not a joke at all. My friend and colleague Carey Casey, the CEO of the National Center for Fathering and author of *Championship*

Fathering, knows this scenario very well. His youngest son, Chance, is 13 years younger than his siblings. Chance was born when Carey was a pastor in Chicago, and Carey well remembers some of the comments he and his wife, Melanie, heard about that time gap.

In his daily radio feature, *Today's Father*, Carey said, "People weren't trying to be mean—they just didn't realize what they were saying. Things like, 'What were y'all thinking?' Or, 'I bet you won't make that mistake again.' If you hear something like that long enough, it can get on your nerves."

So a few weeks after Chance was born, Carey took him right up into the pulpit. Standing before the congregation, he held the baby up in his hands and said, "This boy is a gift from God." Then, he talked about some of the things they had heard, and said, "I know you all don't mean bad, but this is a child that God gave us, even at age 41. Through us, God willing, Chance will never ever feel that he was a mistake."

More than 12 years later, Chance has no recollection of any of those events and never heard those jokes or snide comments. You can see how that father's actions put a stop to any damage before it occurred.

In the same radio broadcast, Carey talked about a similar situation occurring at the birth of his wife, Melanie. She had two older sisters, and her father really wanted a boy. Melanie's mom was so convinced she was going to have a boy that they didn't even have any girl names picked out. Without question, Melanie always felt loved and wanted, but for many years there was a nagging sense that her arrival on earth was a cause for disappointment. Not an easy feeling to deal with. Even in a strong, loving Christian family, a child hearing some misinformation or some gossip or an ill-advised joke can suffer harm to their frail ego.

Do you have an "oops" baby? Is your son or daughter the "wrong" sex? Is your child adopted? Maybe you got married because your girlfriend became pregnant. When that truth comes out—and it will—your son or daughter is going to experience a time of guilt and self-doubt. In another scenario, you might drop a casual remark about how your house is too small or you're worried about paying for college. If your kids hear that at the wrong time, those innocent words may cause them to question their value as a human being. Yikes. That is the last thing any kid should ever think.

If there's any chance your son or daughter might be questioning their place in this world, sit them down and tell them how much they are loved, cherished, adored, and worthy of affection. In some cases, you may want to overstate the obvious to make sure they truly understand they're a valued gift from God. In other cases, you may want to seek out professional counseling to make sure the damage doesn't go deeper than you realize.

Scorecards ready? Dad, do you tell your kids you love them? Check. Do you show your kids you love them? Check. Do your kids have the intellectual awareness that they are wanted, they belong, and God has a most excellent plan for their lives? Check, check, and check.

Takeaway

If there is any chance that any of your kids have heard or imagined they might be a "mistake," set them straight ASAP.

"The supreme happiness of life is the conviction that we are loved."
Victor Hugo (1802–1885)

24

Kids Need Their Dad...

To Be Waiting at the Next Bridge

My brother, Mark, and I were Boy Scouts for about three years, and the highlight had to be the canoe/camping trips during which we earned the coveted 50-mile "Afoot and Afloat" award. Paddling and portaging through the Boundary Waters north of Ely, Minnesota, pushed me beyond my comfort level, which is a good place to be for a 12-year-old. Mark and I had such a blast that the two of us retraced the same journey one summer during our college years.

In preparation for that first Canada trip, our troop made a two-day, 35-mile journey down the Fox River from Yorkville to Ottawa, Illinois, where it empties into the Illinois River. That first morning, my dad drove his two sons down to the canoe launch, made sure our life vests were snug, and waved goodbye as the flotilla of a dozen-plus canoes paddled down the mighty Fox. Moving with the current, even the novice paddlers got into a nice rhythm and were making good time. This wasn't exactly a wilderness adventure; we would pass homes, factories, dams, and overpasses along the way.

A mile or two into our journey, the canoes approached a bridge spanning the river. There standing right in the middle of the overpass was our dad. While the other mothers and fathers had left the launch site and headed back to their other obligations for the day, Ken Payleitner had chosen to make one more connection with his two sons. Mark and I were surprised and delighted to see him. As memory serves, he didn't shout instructions or embarrass us. He just waved as our canoes passed beneath the concrete overpass. Why was he there? Maybe he wanted to make sure we were safe. Maybe he was relieving his guilt for not volunteering to be one of the adult supervisors. Maybe he just wanted to connect with his boys. In any case, it was a nice touch.

Then things began to get interesting. Several miles later, dad was at the next overpass. And the next. And the next. I don't remember how much time elapsed between bridges. I don't know how fast he drove to get to the next bridge or how long he waited. And, I don't remember exactly how many bridges he was on. But it began to be a game. Our canoes would round a bend in the river, we'd catch a glimpse of an overpass in the distance, and a handful of scouts would strain to see if Mr. Payleitner was waiting. There he was. As for me, I was glad that much-heralded figure was my dad.

Of course, there was a bit of a disappointment among the canoeists when we finally came to a bridge on which he was not waiting. That's the risk when you start playing that kind of game. But Dad, that shouldn't keep you from playing. My father's entire investment was probably an hour of time and a quarter tank of gas. Clearly it was worth it. As I write this, 40 years later, it still brings a smile.

Allow me to complete the metaphor. This journey called life has all kinds of milestones—bridges to paddle under or checkpoints to pass—including birthdays, graduations, orchestra concerts, championship games, and award ceremonies. If you make those big events, give yourself a gold star. But then ask yourself, *Isn't that pretty much the bare minimum?* Any dad reading this book is already making the statement that he wants to do a little more than average. Don't you want to do more than just show up? More than just drop and go? A small investment of time and energy—like waiting on the next bridge—can make all the difference.

Examples? Come home early from work and meet your second-grader at the bus stop. Sit up front at the preschool graduation (attended mostly by moms). Chaperone a field trip. Chaperone an overnight field trip. Get to the middle-school games that often start mid-afternoon. Join the WATCH D.O.G.S. (Dads of Great Students) at your kid's elementary school. (If they don't have a WATCH D.O.G.S program, start one and help other dads be heroes too.) Offer to escort a carload of ten-year-olds to the midnight showing of the latest age-appropriate must-see blockbuster. Rinse towels at the car wash fundraiser. Deliver a surprise pizza to your teenager's late-night study session. Drive to your son's college campus to watch an intramural flag football game. Notice that most of the time, no words need be spoken. But your action—just being there—might make an impact that lasts forever.

Another way to think of it is this: Look at what all the other dads are doing, and just do a little bit more. It's not a competition, but "waiting at the next bridge" provides an opportunity for your son or daughter to say with pride, "That's my dad." Even if they don't say it out loud.

Takeaway

Whatever your kid is involved in, you be involved too. Then look for an opportunity to do just a little bit more. Be creative. Be unobtrusive. Be humble. Be there.

> *"Don't wait for extraordinary circumstance to*
> *do good; try to use ordinary situations."*
> CHARLES RICHTER (1900–1985)

#25

Kids Need Their Dad...

To Buy Them a Unicycle

t's okay that no one has ever ridden the unicycle hanging from the ceiling in our garage. Really, it is.

We bought it for Randy's ninth birthday for about 75 bucks. He gave it a try, spending maybe six or eight hours goofing with it. His brothers and sister also spent various amounts of time experimenting with the one-wheeled contraption. Isaac probably stayed up the longest—eight or ten seconds. None of them ever really got the hang of it, and the unicycle now hangs in the corner of the garage as a memorial to "druthers."

Now, I am absolutely sure that out of my five children, one or two had the physical agility and mental acuity to become an expert unicyclist. Again, it's not easy. It would have taken hours of practice, perhaps an entire summer. I certainly am not going to blame any of my kids for not following through. The mental gyroscope required for mastering the unicycle cannot be detected by visual inspection. Plus, I don't think any of them ever caught the vision of how cool it would be to ride down the street on one wheel.

So whether they knew it or not, each of them did a cost-benefit analysis of the time it would take, the amount of frustration they might endure, Dad's expectations, the reality that it might not even be possible, and the immediate and long-term usefulness of having that particular skill. Any of them had the legitimate option to go for it and master it. But each of them chose not to. There was stuff that—at the time—seemed like a better option.

In those pivotal magic summers, during which maturing preteens have few responsibilities and many options, they each decided they "druther" do something else. Their choices were the same choices made by generations of young people: playing catch, swimming, riding two-wheeled bikes, tree-climbing, inventing backyard games, watching the Cubs lose on WGN, tormenting their siblings, hanging out with friends, and maybe even reading a book or two. All reasonable, typical, healthy choices.

In the meantime, the unicycle got pulled out of the garage every once in a while. A garage-exploring neighbor boy would see it and want to give it a try. One or two kids from down the street claimed to be experts, but failed to impress. Now it hangs from the ceiling, just low enough that I bump my head on it once or twice each season.

No regrets. Except that I always wanted to ride a unicycle myself. Yes, in this case, I am guilty of seeking vicarious satisfaction in living by proxy through one of my progeny. But no such luck.

And again, no regrets. Without hesitation, my recommendation to any dad of a nine-year-old is "Buy them a unicycle." The very worst that happens is they are forced to make a choice. Not a failure. Just a choice.

And who knows? Your kid might just master the one-wheeled beast, run away, and join the circus.

Takeaway

All we can do is open doors for our children. They are going to choose to walk through them or not. And that's okay.

"There is much to be said for failure. It is
much more interesting than success."
—MAX BEERBOHM (1872–1956)

26

Kids Need Their Dad...

To Be Their Greatest Cheerleader

Years ago, before I had my own teenagers, I was a volunteer youth leader at my church. I was one of the hip young married guys drafted by the youth pastor to lead small groups and chaperone on overnights. Back then my gifts were a sense of humor, a creative spark, some common sense, and the ability to strum a few guitar chords. Spiritually, I was just slightly more mature than the kids I would oversee. I knew the God of the universe had a plan for me, but I was still trying to figure out my place in this world, not yet knowing that I needed to put him first.

Every Wednesday night, Rita would seclude herself upstairs with toddler Alec and baby Randy for 90 minutes while a dozen high-school students joined me to sit around our living room trying to make sense of life. One evening, I threw out an icebreaker question: "What do you think your life will be like ten years from now?" (It's a good idea to have teenagers think about the future.) Their answers were typical. "A good job." "Probably married." "Definitely not married." "Living in Chicago." I nodded my head and went around the room with the same question. One young man, a little rough around the edges, said, "Professional golfer." My abrupt, thoughtless reply was, "No, seriously."

Well, that was the exact wrong response. I had dismissed his dream. I took a moment that could have been inspiring to everyone in that room, and I blew it. What's more, that young man never cared about anything I said for the rest of the school year. I lost him. I should have said, "That is so cool. Go for it. I'll be looking for your name in the sports pages. I hope you'll remember us when you're on the pro tour." Instead, I crushed his spirit. Even as I said it, I could see his eyes go empty and the wall go up.

Certainly, I was not the only adult influence in his life, but he very likely valued my opinion more than I had realized. Teen boys often will put a 20-something male on a pedestal, and that is a responsibility not to be taken lightly. I've lost track of that young man, and he may not even remember the incident, but it made a profound impact on my life.

From that moment on, I committed myself to become an encourager. With my own kids and their peers, I attempt to help young people see their unlimited potential. Sometimes I go a little too far, raising expectations beyond what might be reasonable. Sometimes I see wasted potential or lost opportunities and make the mistake of pointing out the obvious. But my sincere goal is always to encourage. I recommend you try it.

When the kids are younger, it's a lot easier. Whether it's sports, music, art, spelling bees, chess competitions, or Scout jamborees. Just put a smile in your voice and say, "I think you can do this" or, "Give it your best shot."

As they get older, authentic encouragement has to be based in the reality of goals and circumstance. If you encourage your child to audition for a play, the lead roles may go to the same actors who always land the lead roles. You can encourage their career as a catcher for the high-school team, but there already might be three more experienced catchers on the varsity depth chart. The art-show judge may be a fan of watercolors, but your child works in acrylics. These are all things your child might even know about and not bother to tell you. When you suggest a course of action and your teenager snaps, "Dad, you don't know what you're talking about," they might be right!

Still, Dad, you have a responsibility to supply sincere encouragement, a voice of experience, and other words of wisdom. Do some research in their chosen field of interest. Talk to other parents. When the time is right, ask your son or daughter open-ended questions about their hopes and dreams. Help them to identify open doors and see where they lead.

After an emotional game or performance, the car ride home or the dinner table might be quieter than usual, but really that's okay. It's usually better to say nothing than to extend a cliché such as "Well, at least you gave it a try" or "You'll do better next time." Let them take the lead concerning if and when they want you to perform a postmortem, dissecting and analyzing every aspect of their work. Sometimes they want to talk, sometimes they don't.

It's fascinating that often a young competitor or performer may come away from an effort that seems like a letdown, but they feel quite satisfied with how they did. Conversely, they may have a first-place trophy in hand and feel like they fell far short of their personal goals. An excellent question to ask is, "Did you *do* what you *wanted* to do?" That might launch a good conversation about their approach to the event, their goals, the skills they're trying to improve, and what their next step might be.

The greatest athletes, competitors, artists, craftsmen, and musicians all need to figure out on their own what it takes to be the best they can be. Sometimes they need your help, sometimes they don't. Either way, don't take it personally, because always they need your love and support. At their commencement address, senior banquet, gallery opening, commissioning, inauguration, trophy presentation, Broadway premiere, ribbon-cutting ceremony, or acceptance speech, they'll thank you. I'm sure of it.

Takeaway

Often the best way to encourage your son or daughter is without words. A nod. A handshake. A confident smile. Even a silly thumbs-up. But be ready with praise, suggestions, personal perspective, and a gentle, honest critique when they say, "Dad, what did you think?"

"A mother's encouragement takes away the fear of failure—
confirming you have nothing to lose. A father's encouragement takes
away the fear of victory—confirming you have everything to win."
—Jay K. Payleitner (1957–)

#27

Kids Need Their Dad...

To Throw Out His Porn

There's not a lot of gray area on this matter. Dad, throw away anything resembling pornography. All of it.

Bury deep in your garbage can any magazines with naked or scantily clad women, including all those *Sports Illustrated* swimsuit editions and Victoria's Secret catalogs. Throw away every DVD with an R-rating or worse, unless it really, truly has some socially redeeming value. Shut down your computer until you can install a porn filter and pledge that you will never, ever visit another questionable site or respond to a questionable e-mail solicitation. Purpose in your heart today that you will never again walk into a Hooters restaurant or any other establishment that is in the business of marketing and displaying women as sex objects.

In every one of these areas—magazines, videos, Web surfing, entertainment—draw a line in the sand and do not cross it.

By the way, making these changes is impossible—if you expect to do it under your own power. Men are wired and conditioned to pursue graphic sexual images and, honestly, we are helpless without turning it over to our Creator. We need to ask God for courage and strength. We need to ask God to shield our eyes even as we take that garbage to the trash can. We need to ask God to help us "bounce our eyes" instantly looking away from women with tight or revealing outfits (a technique described in Stephen Arterburn's bestseller *Every Man's Battle*). We need to hold each other accountable to "flee from sexual immorality."

Why? Submitting to the power of pornography prevents you from enjoying healthy relationships with women. It steals your time and attention, keeping you from fulfilling God's plan for your life. It erases your testimony. It finances a trillion-dollar industry that should sicken your stomach. Maybe worst of all, it robs you of a chance to fully devote yourself to God.

Need more persuading? Imagine dying tomorrow. Then picture your loved ones finding that stash of pornography under your bed or in the back of your cabinet. Imagine your wife, boss, mother, son, or daughter reviewing your credit-card bills or checking the log of your recent Web activity. Imagine Jesus hanging out with you for the past week.

Dad—for your family, for your future, for your soul—throw out your porn.*

Takeaway

For your sons, model respect for women. For your daughters, teach them about real beauty. For your wife, choose to love her more every year, every decade, every wrinkle, without compromise.

> *"One word frees us of all the weight and
> pain of life: That word is love."*
> —Sophocles (496 BC–406 BC)

---

* The material in this chapter is adapted from Jay Payleitner, *40 Days to Your Best Life for Men* (Colorado Springs: Honor Books, 2002), 48-50. ©2002 Cook Communications Ministries. *40 Days to Your Best Life For Men* by Honor Books. Used with permission. May not be further reproduced. All rights reserved.

28

Kids Need Their Dad...

To Respond with Something Besides "Read a Book" When Kids Say "There's Nothing to Do"

A round mom, most kids have learned not to whine, "I'm soooo bored. There's nothing to do." They are well aware mom will bury them with household chores like "Empty the dishwasher," "Vacuum the living room," or "Do a load of laundry."

But Dad, your job is to have a much more creative and motivating answer. If you don't, your kids are going to end up wasting precious hours of their life watching TV, playing video games, and staying way clear of Mom.

I suggest you suggest...

Fly a kite. Build a kite. Build a model rocket. Write a book. Write a poem. Plant a tree. Bait a hook. Bake some cookies. Bake some apples (cored, filled with cinnamon, wrapped in foil). Play checkers. Play chess. Play speed chess. Invent a new game with checkers. Jump rope. Play hopscotch. Play rock, scissors, paper. Teach rock, scissors, paper to a four-year-old. Invent a new app for your iPhone. Go to the library. Learn the Dewey Decimal System. Start a business. Design a business card. Put on a puppet show. Cut paper snowflakes. Make a mix CD for your favorite uncle. Get a big jar, fill it with sand and ants for a homemade ant farm. Drop a donut next to an anthill and see what happens. Visit Grandma. Visit the older lady down the street. Visit a cemetery. Mow the grass. Trim the hedges. Throw a tea party. Play 20 questions. Think up 20 great tweets, then join Twitter with something worth saying. Start a blog. Fix the fence. Build a shelf. Carve a bar of soap.

Carve a potato. Play Frisbee. Play Ultimate Frisbee. Lay out a Frisbee golf course in your neighborhood. Find the most awesome Psalm. Memorize it. Make a huge tub of homemade bubble solution (two-thirds of a cup of Joy or Dawn, one gallon cold water, three tablespoons of glycerin or light corn syrup) and then fashion a giant bubble wand out of a coat hanger or even a hula hoop. Find a pen pal. Fill a photo album. See what's under the couch cushions. Sweep the front sidewalk. Wash the car. Wash your bike. Wash the dog. Play kick the can or ghost in the graveyard. Play capture the flag. Play spud. Play home-run derby or Peggy roll up. Find a long plastic tarp, add dishwashing liquid and a garden hose, and make a giant slip 'n' slide. Make an animated cartoon by drawing stick figures on the bottom of consecutive pages of a pad of paper. Do leaf rubbings. Do gravestone rubbings. Identify birds. Climb a tree. Think up an animal beginning with every letter of the alphabet. Make a tie-dye T-shirt. Paper airplanes. Origami. Hacky Sack. Harass a sibling. Practice shuffling cards. Learn a magic trick. Play Candy Land with your little sister. Do math worksheets (yikes!). Play hide-and-seek. Play sardines. Make a tent out of blankets. Collect some bugs. Make a campfire. Memorize the presidents. Then recite them as fast as you can. Learn the Greek alphabet. Learn the American Sign Language alphabet.

Worth noting: Don't let age be a limitation. Those alphabet ideas were accomplished by our eldest, Alec, before kindergarten. By second grade he could recite the presidents in under nine seconds.

Of course, the list is really endless. But every year it gets harder and harder to pry kids away from the old electronic standbys. It might cause a short-term mutiny in your home, but I totally recommend unplugging that TV or banning video games for a week or a month and seeing what transpires. They may never go back! (My small-group leader, Dave, has unplugged the family television for almost the entire summer the last four years—so it can be done.)

Takeaway

Despite this wonderful list, understand that most of the time your kids don't want your ideas, they want you.

"Before I got married I had six theories about raising children; now, I have six children and no theories."
—John Wilmot (1647–1680)

29

Kids Need Their Dad...

To See Who They Really Are

Many young people *think too highly of themselves.* They believe the world owes them big-time. Why does that happen to some kids and not others? Perhaps it was because they've had it too easy growing up. Mom (or a maid) picked up their clothes. Dad never said no. Maybe they are just so beautiful and so clever that the world around them simply falls at their feet. Maybe it just happens. In any case, you probably agree that kids like that need a dose of humility and appreciation for what they have. A severe cutback in privileges may be in order. A mission trip to a third-world nation or a summer of dirty, sweaty, exhausting work might be exactly what they need to find their place in this world.

Just as many young people *don't understand how wonderful they are.* They live a pained existence that doesn't seem to have much purpose. Why does that happen to some kids and not others? Perhaps they experienced physical or emotional abuse as a child. Mom didn't hold them. Dad was too busy or too brutal. Never a kind word was said. Maybe they are just so filled with fear, depression, and anxiety that they see no hope for the future. Maybe it just happens. In any case, you probably agree that kids like that need a healthy dose of encouragement and recognition that they possess many undiscovered gifts. A hug and a fresh start may be in order. Some time with a caring counselor or compassionate advocate might be exactly what they need to help them find their place in this world.

Of course, all kids need both. They need to see life as a gift *and* a challenge. They need to feel beautiful *and* useful. They need to feel wise *and* wanted. These needs are universal. Not bound by economic status, IQ, athletic ability, race, sex, or religious background.

This is not about suicide prevention, but it could be. This not an anti-abortion message, but it could be that too. This is about helping our kids discover the answer to the question "What is the value of a life?" Scientists tell us we are 98 percent water and the rest of the elements in our physical bodies are worth less than a buck. Hopefully, we are not judged on our chemical makeup.

The true value of something is not really about cash. Value is determined by identifying something for which it can be exchanged. A cup of fancy coffee at Starbucks costs about what you'd pay for a new baseball. The cost of a sunroom addition is about what you'd pay for a Lexus or for a single year at an Ivy League school.

So what is the value of your child's life? Dad, I know you would die for your child. If a decision had to be made, you would exchange your life for his or hers, right? Do they know that? If you tell them how much they really mean to you, it just might make a difference in your relationship. After all, you're a valuable guy, right?

Let me go a giant step further. Someone has already demonstrated the exact value of your child by trading his life for theirs. That's right—your child is worth Jesus. Theologians sometimes even call Jesus' substitutionary death "the great exchange." As a matter of fact, you need to let your child know that if he or she was the only person who ever lived, Jesus loves them so much that he would have died on the cross to pay the penalty for their sins.

One of the most accurate descriptions of Jesus is "servant king." He died to serve. He lives to reign. As the ultimate role model, Jesus also has the answer to both kinds of adolescent attitudes.

Young persons who are thinking a little too highly of themselves need to be reminded that at the Last Supper, Jesus took a basin of water and washed the feet of the disciples. They would also do well to read this reminder from the Gospels:

> Whoever wants to become great among you must be your servant,
> and whoever wants to be first must be your slave—just as the Son
> of Man did not come to be served, but to serve, and to give his life
> as a ransom for many" (Matthew 20:26-28).

Young persons who are thinking too poorly of themselves need to be reminded they can be an heir to God's kingdom. It's not because of anything they can do, it's because of what Jesus' love and mercy have already done.

> He saved us, not because of righteous things we had done, but because of his mercy. He saved us through the washing of rebirth and renewal by the Holy Spirit, whom he poured out on us generously through Jesus Christ our Savior, so that, having been justified by his grace, we might become heirs having the hope of eternal life (Titus 3:5-7).

Takeaway

Not only young people, but grown men also have a hard time balancing ego and humility. It's not easy to acknowledge our sinful condition. On the other hand, it's also not easy to understand how God could love someone like us. We need to trust that God knows who we really are and has a wonderful plan for our life.

> *"Jesus is the God whom we can approach without pride and before whom we can humble ourselves without despair."*
> —BLAISE PASCAL (1623–1662)

30

Kids Need Their Dad...

To Run Through a Vacation Checklist in the Driveway

My family doesn't groan anymore when I run through my verbal checklist as we leave the driveway and travel the first few blocks on an overnight or weeklong adventure. Over the years, each of them (including Rita) has said, "Oops! Stop. We gotta go back."

I no longer have to say, "See—aren't you glad for my vacation checklist?" They know I'm right. It's one of those rare, small moments I get to savor while claiming victory for dads everywhere.

As a public service to dads and families, following is my vacation checklist. Like everything else in this book, take what you like, leave what you don't, and make it your own. Here it is in no mandatory order:

Cell phones. Chargers. Wallets. Purses. Glasses. Prescriptions. Sunglasses. Laptops. Computer cords. Keys. Watches. Maps. Directions. Credit cards. Coupons. Shoes. Socks. Hanging clothes. Belts. Sunscreen. Swimsuits. Towels. Hats. Gifts. Pillows. Blankets. "Rags." (That's Rae Anne's stuffed dog.) Deodorant. Girls' stuff. Shaving kits. Clean underwear. Reading material. Munchies for the car.

Say it fast before you get too far from home. The list varies depending on destination—beach vacations versus out-of-town weddings versus camping trips. The list also comes in handy as we leave hotels and beach houses heading for home. You'll notice that the more important items are mentioned early and many of the items kind of go in pairs. Once you start mentioning items that you can pick up cheap at any drugstore, then you can stop talking.

Try it on your next trip. Sooner or later, you'll be a hero for rescuing an entire journey. The one potential problem is that the family starts to expect it. I am just waiting for the day when I rattle off my vacation checklist and happen to forget one item, and that one item—of course—is the one that's forgotten. Somehow, I'll be the one taking the blame.

Takeaway

Sometimes dads say or do things that get automatic eye rolls or groans from their kids. Don't let that stop you. If you believe in what you're doing, keep doing it.

"Though we travel the world over to find the beautiful,
we must carry it with us or we find it not."
—RALPH WALDO EMERSON (1803–1882)

31

Kids Need Their Dad...

To Make Sure His Brain Is Engaged Before Putting His Mouth in Gear

Conventional wisdom suggests men may not gossip like women, but we have our own damaging way of using words. Most of our foot-in-mouth experiences come out of our tendency to pretty much say whatever comes to our mind.

The consequences of not holding your tongue can be severe. You can lose your job for lying or harassing. Sarcasm and bragging will keep your friends at a distance. Angry words demoralize and embarrass both the speaker and the listener. Words that belittle, accuse, or nitpick will damage your family relationships. Jokes about your young daughter's eating habits may lead to a serious case of anorexia during her teenage years. You can build your son up or tear him down with a mere handful of words.

I will never forget a brief conversation I had with my dad my junior year of high school after taking first place in a junior-varsity wrestling tournament. The trophy was small, but I had fought hard to earn it. He held it in his hand and said, "Maybe next year you can win a varsity trophy." Now, of course, he meant it as a challenge to keep working hard and reach for the stars. But at that moment, his words cut me like a knife. The Bible has a great teaching—especially appropriate for dads—on this matter. "Rejoice with those who rejoice; mourn with those who mourn" (Romans 12:15). When one of your children comes to you with emotional news, your best response is to reflect their demeanor right back to them. In the moment, celebrate in their joy or join them in their sorrow. Use phrases like "That's fantastic" or

"Oh, man, I'm so sorry." There's plenty of time for advice, correction, planning, or personal challenges a little later on. Whenever possible, laugh or cry right along with the people you care about most.*

Another story: Back when my son, Alec, became grass-cutting age, I turned him loose on our bumpy backyard with our rickety old lawnmower. About halfway through the job, he stopped the project and called me out to assess a problem. It seems one of the bolts holding the right front wheel assembly had worked itself loose and was now lying somewhere in the backyard. Over the past several weeks, I had tightened that bolt several times; it had a tendency to rattle itself loose, but I always caught it just in time. Had I warned Alec about it? No. Had I secured that bolt in place extra tightly before turning the lawnmower over to my rookie grass cutter? No. Was it pretty much my fault that the right front wheel collapsed and the bolt was now lost? Yes.

How did this young dad respond? It was not pretty. Looking back, I was obviously angry with myself and took it out on poor Alec. It was almost 20 years ago, but I still recall my exact words. I said, "Son, you have got to be more aware of your surroundings!" Yow. What does that mean? Was I blaming a ten-year-old boy for not noticing a loose bolt on the wheel of a lawnmower? What an idiot I was.

The good news is that God has since convicted me of my wicked tongue. I think about that day just about every time I mow the lawn. Five lawnmowers and two backyards later, I still look down and see all the bolts and connections that have the potential to rattle loose...and I wonder what I was thinking. I don't beat myself up about it anymore—it's just a regular reminder of how even a well-intentioned dad can mess up.

The end of the story is that Alec and I have had a few good conversations and several good laughs over the incident in recent years. He remembers the entire incident very well and doesn't hesitate to point out how—as instructed—he has taught himself to be sometimes *too* "aware of his surroundings." He didn't turn into an obsessive-compulsive, but his attention to detail sometimes goes a little too far. Such is the power of a father's words to a young boy.

Have worse things come out of my mouth since then? Yes, regretfully. But I don't dare put that down here for the world to read. God and I are still working on my tendency to say whatever comes to mind.

Worth noting: The Bible also has some great teaching about a loose tongue and acknowledges that choosing the right words is a constant battle: "Out of the same mouth come praise and cursing" (James 3:10). Still, there is a reward for those who can control their words: "He who guards his mouth and his tongue, guards his soul from troubles" (Proverbs 21:23 NASB).

Takeaway

Understand the power of a father's words. Don't sit silently in fear of saying something you may later regret. Instead, practice the art of picking and polishing your words a little more carefully.

"A word aptly spoken is like apples of gold in settings of silver."
—PROVERBS 25:11

Kids Need Their Dad...

To Not Yell About Spilled Milk

Accidents happen. Kids spill their milk. They know they messed up. They're already sorry. Yelling at them will not improve the situation. Yelling will only make it worse. When the milk glass tumbles, your best course of action is to throw napkins at the spill, make efficient use of anything absorbent, and keep repeating, "No problem. No problem." (Make sure you sponge up all the milk from any carpet, because sour milk smells pretty nasty after about three days.)

After the dining room settles down there are several courses of action to take. Certainly, you may want to reassess the size and shape of drinking cups you use. (Although you don't want to humiliate a seven-year-old by making him go back to using a sippy cup.) You may want to quietly pour smaller portions for a while. You may also want to keep a roll of paper towels within reach. But what you don't want to do is make a big serious deal about it. Like I said, accidents happen.

Laughing it off is actually a pretty wise option. During the entire decade of the 1990s, my wife regularly threatened the boys with charm school. An excellent dad response would be to recall embarrassing moments in your own life when you dipped your tie into the gravy boat or tucked the tablecloth into your pants and pulled the entire table setting onto your lap. Make something up if you have to—the more outlandish the better. Then let them know you still expect them to be a little more careful.

We want our kids to believe that when something bad happens, Dad makes it better. If it's something minor like spilled milk, Dad will make it all go away. If it's more serious, Dad will help fix it, tow it, restore it, minimize the damage, or stand beside me as I face the music. Yes, there will be reper-cussions. If damage was done, Dad is not going to let me get away without paying some kind of price. But I trust him. Dad will provide a voice of rea-son and bring calm to the storm.

Unfortunately, some dads rage when their kids mess up. It begins with yelling "What's wrong with you!" after a glass tips at the dinner table. And it just gets worse. Raging is always counterproductive. It drives the culprit away. It reinforces the idea that bringing a problem to Dad is a bad idea and will just make matters worse. What happens then? The next time there's a mess that needs straightening, Dad never finds out.

Does that sound like a good thing? It most definitely is not. Until your children are well into adulthood, one of your most important jobs is to help guide them through the dark tunnels and thorny paths of life.

It begins with small things. Spilled milk? No problem. Broken window? Let's head to the hardware store. A crack in mom's favorite vase? Let's go tell her together.

Then it gets more complex. The older kid at the bus stop is picking a fight with your son. Your son slams the cat in the car door. He's getting a D in algebra. He rolls the Volkswagen onto its roof on a highway exit ramp during his early morning delivery job. His girlfriend breaks his heart. (All of which happened to me.)

Kids of any age need to be able to pick up their cell phone and call Dad. When you get that call, Dad, be thankful. They could have called someone else, but you have earned their trust. They know you will rise to the occa-sion and be the dad. Maybe later, you will deliver a short lecture, insist on an apology, or require some financial restitution, but for now you are the hero of the moment.

With all the serious life challenges that lie ahead for your kids, doesn't it seem trivial to raise your voice over a little puddle of milk? What really matters is your relationship and making things right. When faced with any problem at any time, you need to be able to say, "I love you. It'll be okay. We'll get through this together."

Can you do that? Do you have the courage to commit to that response no matter what? Here's a test then. What would be your initial response to these statements from one of your kids?

"Dad, I wrecked the car."

"Dad, I'm dropping out of school."

"Dad, I'm at the police station."

"Dad, I'm pregnant."

"Dad, my girlfriend is pregnant."

Yes, you need to get all the facts. Yes, you need to make sure the punishment fits the crime. Yes, you need to help meet all short-term needs while keeping the future in mind. But the core message of how you respond needs to be "I love you. It'll be okay. We'll get through this together."

Takeaway

Didn't you always want to be a superhero? Superman. Batman. A knight in shining armor. Your kids will give you that chance and it won't be make-believe. You'll be a real-life hero. But only if they trust you not to yell, persecute, abuse, or jump to unfair conclusions.

> *"Parents are heroes already—all they have to do is start acting like it."*
> —Josh McDowell

#33

Kids Need Their Dad...

To Freak Out a Little When They Lose His Socket Wrench Set

I'm assuming you own a socket wrench set. If you don't, get one soon. It is an absolute requirement for certain maintenance and construction projects. Plus, this chapter will make a lot more sense to someone who owns a set of socket wrenches. You can get a sweet set for less than 50 bucks.

Anyway. Someday soon—if it hasn't happened already—one of your angelic, innocent children is going to borrow your socket wrench set and not put it back. Sometime later, you're going to need that socket wrench set to assemble a floor lamp, adjust a bicycle wheel, or tighten a miscellaneous bolt. Whistling while you work, you'll make your way over to the place where you always, always keep the socket wrench set. Lo and behold, it will not be there. Perhaps even worse, it *will* be there, and when you open the case to get just the right socket, the particular socket you seek won't be there. What's more, several of the other sockets will not be there either. You'll know this because several of the little precast indentations in the case that are designed to organize and categorize the sockets will be empty.

For most dads, this is our signal to freak out. It's a natural human response. Sometimes, things happen that make us angry. When that happens you have two choices. Turning it into a bad thing by losing it. Or turning it into a good thing by keeping your cool.

If you lose it—by stomping, cursing, accusing, wailing—you lose a little piece of yourself. You will be surrendering a small portion of your authority and credibility as a father. If your kids are small, they may actually be frightened by your loss of control. If your kids are older, you will be giving them permission to lose their cool when they face moments of frustration in their own lives. Plus, in the future when you tell them to "calm down" about some minor issue, they will always have this thought in the back of their heads: "Sure, old man, why don't you practice what you preach!" Ouch.

Still, your socket wrench is missing. You are frustrated. Your kids need to learn to respect other people's property. Something has to be done!

Here's my suggestion: Proceed with the freak-out process. But just a little. No swearing. No throwing things. No yelling. To be clear, under these circumstances it is perfectly acceptable and even expected for you to walk (not stomp) around the house and ask in a firm but controlled manner, "Has anyone seen my socket wrench set?" or "Who was using my socket wrench set?"

Do not expect an answer. If you do get an answer, it will always be the same two words. "Not me." Or perhaps some variation of these four words, "I didn't touch it." At this point, please, Dad, do not escalate the amount of freaking out. It's tempting, I know, but you will regret it. Take it from a man who has experienced both extremes. An *out-of-control* freak-out will fill you with regret and remorse. A *controlled* freak-out is a beautiful thing.

Ephesians 4:26 lays it out in a mere six words, "In your anger do not sin."

A controlled freak-out can accomplish several objectives. First, you get their attention. Second, they take you seriously. Third, you might actually stir their brain cells and induce them to remember where they inadvertently left your socket wrench set. Fourth, you demonstrate that it is possible to feel intense frustration and retain self-control and composure.

It's worth repeating. If you exhibit any kind of rabid, maniacal, or volcanic behavior, you have lost respect, lost influence, and probably lost your socket wrench set forever.

For the record, all of the above applies to other tools, athletic equipment, car keys, office supplies, television remotes, flashlights, cell phones, rolls of duct tape, toilet plungers, sports sections, road maps, and "the good scissors."

In the end, your children's ability to deal with the inevitable teeny-tiny frustrations of life like a mature adult is more important than any lost, stolen, or misplaced item. That's a lesson you can talk about until your face turns blue, but it won't sink in. However, if you can model that key moment of composure without your face turning red, then your kids may just get the message.

Takeaway

Know the difference between self-serving anger and righteous anger. Even Jesus got angry, turning over the tables of the money changers in the temple. His motivation was just. His actions were focused. His goal was to honor God.

> *"Everyone should be quick to listen, slow to speak and slow to become angry, for man's anger does not bring about the righteous life that God desires."*
>
> —JAMES 1:19-20

34

Kids Need Their Dad...

To Teach Them the World's Greatest Knock-Knock Joke

First, Dad, you should probably know the history of the knock-knock joke. But since that history is a little murky, I'm just going to make something up. Okay?

Early knock-knock jokes were based on real-life names of people who might actually come to your front door. Examples:

> Knock-knock.
> *Who's there?*
> Justin.
> *Justin who?*
> Justin time! I thought you weren't home.

> Knock-knock.
> *Who's there?*
> Isabel.
> *Isabel who?*
> Isabel working? I had to knock.

It wasn't long before the punch line had nothing to do with someone standing at a door. Knock-knock jokes became just an excuse for making a pun out of people's first names:

> Knock-knock.
> *Who's there?*

Dwayne.
Dwayne who?
Dwayne the bathtub, I'm dwowning.

Knock-knock.
Who's there?
Sarah.
Sarah who?
Sarah doctor in the house?

After decades of knock-knock jokes based solely on names, somehow it all changed. The person doing the knocking didn't have to be a person. The trigger word could be a vegetable, an article of clothing, or anything really:

Knock-knock.
Who's there?
Lettuce.
Lettuce who?
Lettuce in, it's cold out here.

Knock-knock.
Who's there?
Radio.
Radio who?
Radio not. Here I come.

Knock-knock.
Who's there?
Wooden shoe.
Wooden shoe who?
Wooden shoe like to know?

The next generation of knock-knock jokes had songs for the punch line. Usually classic folksongs or show tunes:

Knock-knock.
Who's there?
Freeze.
Freeze who?
Freeze a jolly good fellow, freeze a jolly good fellow...

Knock-knock.
Who's there?
Sam and Janet.
Sam and Janet who?
Sam and Janet evening, you may find a stranger…

Knock-knock.
Who's there?
Aardvark.
Aardvark who?
Aardvark a million miles for one of your smiles…

Then the entire knock-knock joke world was turned upside down when joke tellers began to incorporate the "who" part of the response into the punch line. That idea gave new life to the genre.

Knock-knock.
Who's there?
Boo.
Boo who?
Well, it's only a joke. You don't have to cry about it.

Knock-knock.
Who's there?
Hatch.
Hatch who?
Gesundheit.

Knock-knock.
Who's there?
Little old lady.
Little old lady who?
Wow! I didn't know you could yodel.

No chapter on knock-knock jokes can be complete without this classic that you know and love.

Knock-knock.
Who's there?
Banana.

Banana who?
Knock-knock.
Who's there?
Banana.
Banana who?
Knock-knock.
Who's there?
Banana.
Banana who?
Knock-knock.
Who's there?
Orange.
Orange who?
Orange you glad I didn't say "banana" again?

Finally, here is the greatest knock-knock joke of all time. Unfortunately it doesn't come across very well on the printed page. But try it out on someone you love and see how well it works.

Knock-knock.
Who's there?
Interrupting cow.
Interrupting—?
MOO!

The word "moo" is funny all by itself, but if you say it before they finish their response, the effect is pretty amusing. Try saying it loud or soft. It works both ways.

A few more words about knock-knock jokes before you go try them out on your kids.

First, it's a total blast to teach them to a two- or three-year-old, even before their verbal skills and sense of irony are developed. You laugh and so they laugh and then you laugh some more. Later, when they do finally understand the wordplay in one of the jokes, their eyes get real big, and you can actually witness a whole new world opening to them.

Second, once you wind them up, they won't stop.

The Internet is a never ending source of knock-knock jokes. Unfortunately, most are distasteful or just not very funny or clever. Still, Web sites filled with jokes and riddles can be a valuable resource for fathers, but as with everything on the Web, you need to use your discretion and judgment.

Knock-knock.
Who's there?
Woodshop.
Woodshop who?
Woodshop put this book down and go tell your kid a joke!

Takeaway

The next person you see, tell them a knock-knock joke. Or two.

"You don't stop laughing because you grow old. You grow old because you stop laughing."

—Michael Pritchard

Kids Need Their Dad...

To Apply the Brakes on Slippery Slopes

This chapter might not make it past the Harvest House editors because I'm about to type the word *crap*. There, I did it. Does that shock you? Probably not. You're a big boy and you've heard that word before—and much worse. So have your kids.

More critical than whether or not to include such a word in this book is this question: "Will you—or do you—allow that four-letter word to be used *in your home*?"

In my quest to be the best father possible and promote godly fathering, I asked that exact question of 20 veteran Christian dads whose opinions I respect. These are guys who I knew would shoot straight with me. Their replies via e-mail were enlightening, and I am grateful for their honest words, which I promised would remain anonymous.

A few dads reluctantly had decided to tolerate the use of that word in their homes, hoping that would be the worst of it. Others admitted—with some remorse—to using it themselves. The general consensus was that as Christian men and leaders of our families we need to commit ourselves and challenge our kids to a higher standard. This particular word may not present a moral issue, but language is an obvious way to separate who we are and what we stand for compared with the rest of the culture.

The thoughtful responses of these 20 guys left me with other insights worth passing on. Several dads specifically emphasized that too many Christian homes think nothing of allowing other raunchy expressions like "this sucks" or "pissed off." Especially disturbing is the casual use of the Lord's name as an expletive or expression of amazement. Clearly, the standards for our families cannot be the same as our children's classmates or network television producers. A trusted friend wrote, "One reason I gave up watching *Extreme Home Makeover* was the near-fire-hose use of 'Oh my God' by the recipients of the new home."

At a couple homes, "shoot" and "darn" are not allowed because of their origin in other more vulgar terms. (That's an impressive stand to take. I salute those men.)

In a few e-mail responses I was reminded of the "beauty of the English language" and challenged that this topic is a chance to "teach our kids to elevate their speech." Several guys suggested that "context is key," which might leave some gray area, but allows room for discussion and reasoned debate—especially with older kids. I also was appreciative of two on-target biblical references I received from my friends.

> Whatever you do, whether in word or deed, do it all in the name of the Lord Jesus, giving thanks to God the Father through him (Colossians 3:17).

> Brothers, whatever is true, whatever is noble, whatever is right, whatever is pure, whatever is lovely, whatever is admirable—if anything is excellent or praiseworthy—think about such things (Philippians 4:8).

The net-net is that we need to keep our family standards high and be able to tell our children why. Too often, we just let these kinds of decisions evolve without drawing hard lines or challenging our kids to make wiser choices. Believe me, I am not the right guy to tell any dad where to draw the line on language. But since you asked, the S-word should probably be considered going too far, and you can use your own good judgment from there.

When it comes to coarse language, there's something comforting about drawing a line *before* the word in question comes up. That way you don't have to make a snap decision on the spot. When Junior spouts his first innocent expletive, Mom and Dad don't have to look at each other in terror and decide how to respond. You already have the response worked out—"Young man, let me be clear. You cannot use that word in this house. As a matter of fact, you cannot use it anywhere else either. It's vulgar. It dishonors God. It dishonors this family. It makes you look foolish. Besides, there are so many other great words to use. By the way, if you ever hear me use the word, it's still wrong. And you can expect an apology from me."

The early stages of potty mouth are really just another slippery slope from which we need to rescue our children. If we laugh when the preschooler says "poop," then they're going to try another word. And another. And another. Let's grab hold of them at the top of the slope and keep them from descending into the slime. With little ones, set the standard early. With older kids, you may want to throw the topic out for discussion. See if you can come up with standards for your entire family and agree to hold each other accountable. (Yikes—that means you too, Dad.)

Oh by the way, if your kids are in kindergarten or younger, now would be a good time for you and your bride to set standards for a wide variety of issues that may seem trivial and far off in the future. Establish those rules early and you are way ahead of the game. Potential explosive topics include movie ratings, TV viewing, graphic video games, your daughter's wardrobe, the use of alcohol, swimsuit issues in sports magazines, magazines for sexy single gals, tattoos, piercings, smoking, curfews, and anything else you can think of. You may think your kids are immune to some of these issues. That might be true, but don't count on it.

Dad, don't be afraid to draw the line. At the same time, be careful about delivering ultimatums, because they can backfire on you. If you decree that your children cannot live in your house if they get a tattoo, what happens when your daughter gets a cute little butterfly on her ankle? Do you kick her out? Still, you do want to make your expectations known.

Your kids need—and want—your help to make many of these decisions. The way you have raised them, they already understand the concept of good choices and bad choices. What they don't realize is how easily one teeny, tiny bad choice leads to another. In C.S. Lewis' wonderful book *The Screwtape Letters*, the diabolical elder demon pens some wise advice to his apprentice, advocating the effectiveness of the slippery slope. Uncle Screwtape writes, "The safest road to Hell is the gradual one. This is the road taken by quiet people, responsible citizens, religious people, our neighbors and even people participating in the Christian church."

--- **Takeaway** ---

In the grand scheme of fathering, there are many surprises. Young people testing their tongues is not one of them. You know it's coming. Draw some lines now to help your kids choose their words wisely. And Dad, you do the same.

*"They may look small and insignificant, but mind
what I say, resist them—make no compromise, let no
sin lodge quietly and undisturbed in your heart."*
—J.C. Ryle (1816–1900)

Kids Need Their Dad...

To Make a Pair of Homemade Stilts

D ad, even if you're not handy in the woodworking department, I've got a worthy project for you and your six- to ten-year-old. It's cheap, easy, and doable in a single relaxing afternoon. Plus, it's something they'll actually use, not just stick on a shelf. It's stilts.

Trust me. Kids love the idea of being taller than they are. A couple things before you get started. First, I'm not recommending you go out and purchase professional stilts made of aluminum and plastic that attach to special shoes. I'm talking about the kind of old fashioned stilts dads and kids have been making for generations out of leftover wood they find in their garages. Second, if you hammer your thumb or drill through your hand or if your kid breaks his wrist falling from a foot and half off the ground, it's not my fault. You're the dad, you're in charge. So no lawsuits, okay?

Really, this is a piece of cake. I'll try to explain it, but if you go online and Google "homemade wooden stilts" you'll find dad-friendly instructions with helpful illustrations. (Two Web sites I found are diylife.com or dangerouslyfun.com/stilts.) A trip to the library may also add to the shared adventure. (Check out 684.08 in the Dewey Decimal System. While you're at it, explain what the Dewey Decimal System is to your kids. If you don't know, ask a librarian!)

Each stilt is actually just two pieces of wood. The long piece could be some 1 x 2 wood trim about 6 or 7 feet long. The other piece is the footrest. A triangle cut out of a scrap of 2 x 4 works. Slap 'em together with screws, bolts, or even nails, and you're done. If you're an experienced carpenter, you're probably two steps ahead of me. That's fine. Just remember not to leave your son or daughter behind. (This is quality time with your kid, okay?) If you're confused, that's also okay. Take the time to figure it out and sketch it out on a yellow pad or the back of your business card. Do the research together.

Really, this shouldn't be an all-day project. Once you get back from the home center, even if you don't have a fancy workshop, it should come together pretty efficiently. My attorneys want me to tell you that my official recommendation on that first pair is to keep the footrests low—about a foot off the ground. You can always make a more challenging pair later.

Finally, how about a quick stilt-walking lesson? The key is to start with the poles under your armpits, straight out, as if you were jousting. You'll be tempted to hold them like ski poles, but that's not proper stilt-walking technique. To control them, you have to hunch over a little and wrap your arms around the poles and hold them with your thumbs pointing down. For a visual reference, again, you may want to head to the Internet. A YouTube search will find you all kinds of videos of guys walking several feet off the ground on a wide variety of stilts. (That will also give you an opportunity to review the proper use of the Internet and how there are all kinds of choices—good and bad—any time you start clicking around on it.)

So get to it, Dad. Remember, this really isn't about researching, designing, shopping, hauling, sawing, nailing, drilling, sanding, screwing, or stilt-walking. It's about you and them. It's about building a family. It's about living life and learning stuff together along the way. Don't worry if the quality of construction is not up to the standards of master carpenters. Don't worry if you bend a nail, drill a few extra holes, or skin a knee collapsing on the driveway. Don't worry if your kids are better stilt-walkers than you. I confess, at this kind of stuff, all my kids are better than me.

Oh yeah, when they do get that 12-inch boost, suddenly your grade-schooler will be looking you right in the eye. That glimpse into the future makes the whole afternoon worthwhile.

Takeaway

Do this. Saturday or Sunday afternoon, just do it. Don't think about it too much. Don't wait for just the right time. Tell your kid to get in the car. Go to the home center, buy some wood, and make a pair of stilts. Why not?

"If you want to build a ship, don't drum up the men to
gather wood, divide the work and give orders. Instead,
teach them to yearn for the vast and endless sea."

—ANTOINE DE SAINT-EXUPÉRY (1900–1944)

To Read Between the Lines of Psalm 127

Will you join me in reading Psalm 127?

> Unless the LORD builds a house,
>   the work of the builders is wasted.
> Unless the LORD protects a city,
>   guarding it with sentries will do no good.
> It is useless for you to work so hard
>   from early morning until late at night,
>   anxiously working for food to eat;
>   for God gives rest to his loved ones.
> Children are a gift from the LORD;
>   they are a reward from him.
> Children born to a young man
>   are like arrows in a warrior's hands.
> How joyful is the man whose quiver is full of them!
> He will not be put to shame
>   when he confronts his accusers at the city gates.
>   —Psalm 127 NLT

It's an amazing passage. Psalm 127. Read it again and check out all the subtext. Because—Dad—it's about you and your family.

Allow me to paraphrase: It says you can work 80-hour weeks building a house and buying food, thinking you're providing for your family, but actually you're neglecting them. It says you can worry and try to protect your kids from all the nasty influences out there, but you can't do it alone. We need to trust God to protect and provide for our family. They all belong to him anyway! Your children are a gift from God. He has specifically empowered and equipped you to guide and direct them like arrows. Not to put any pressure on you, but God is counting on your kids to be a positive influence to future generations. Sending them off to fly straight and true is more important than any other work you do.

If you didn't know it, that pouch on the back of an archer that holds his arrows is called a quiver. And if you have a full quiver—lots of kids—you have a great shot at a life filled with joy. Even better, as you watch your kids grow in God's grace, they will accomplish wonderful things and make you proud. Not so you can boast, but so you can give the glory back to God.

Then, even your enemies downtown by the city gates will have to admit you're not a bad guy. After all, your kids turned out pretty well.

I'm not making this up. It's all in Psalm 127.

Takeaway

Never think of your children as a burden. They are a blessing! A reward! What could possibly be more satisfying than sending a houseful of children off into the world to do great things?

> *"Parents are often so busy with the physical rearing of*
> *children that they miss the glory of parenthood, just as*
> *the grandeur of the trees is lost when raking leaves."*
> —Marcelene Cox (1911–1999)

38

Daughters Need Their Dad...

To Willingly Do the Hokey Pokey, the Macarena, and Even the Chicken Dance

I f you've got a daughter, prepare to boogie. Get ready to make a complete fool of yourself in a public place along with dozens of other dads and daughters. I'm talking, of course, about the "Daddy-Daughter Date Nite" that takes place each year at many park districts, schools, community centers, country clubs, and even churches around the country.

For the uninitiated, here's what you can expect. The events are just dads (and maybe some granddads or uncles) and their daughters up to fifth grade or so. No moms or brothers allowed. The dads wear anything from nice shirts and slacks to tuxedos. The young ladies are dressed in their finest party dresses, hair done just so, wearing all the jewelry they might own. When she was about five, Rae Anne insisted on wearing a princess tiara she had somehow acquired, and that was just fine with me. After raising four court jesters, she was indeed my princess.

You can be as formal and chivalrous as you want, but do consider ringing your own doorbell, pinning on a corsage, posing for pictures, helping with her coat, opening car doors, and just being generally gallant. The event probably does not include dinner, but will have snacks and beverages. Bonus activities may include a magician or clown, balloon animals, complimentary photos, and party favors.

The highlight of the event is the dance itself, 90 minutes of songs you know and love that will have you and your daughter(s) singing along and shaking your booties. Every town seems to have a DJ that specializes in daddy-daughter events, and he knows how to get the crowd moving. The younger girls playfully swing on their daddy's arm or race around the floor. But the older girls—not quite young women—have a certain unspoken wistfulness about them as they know that childhood is coming to an end. The dads know that too. Often this will be the last time they dance together until her wedding reception more than a decade away.

I can't think about "Daddy-Daughter Date Nite" without giving a nod to Terry and Ally Schweizer, who served as double-date partners for Rae Anne and me for several of these annual events. Each year, Terry would pick us up, and invariably the girls would sit in the backseat comparing their jewelry and outfits. The double date worked out well because both Ally and Rae Anne have four brothers, and one-on-one time with Dad is highly coveted.

One key bit of advice for the evening is to stick with your date. At dinner parties with your wife, sometimes the women congregate in one area and the men circle up in another. But this is a rare daddy-daughter event—you can catch up with the other dads some other time. Also, I suggest you mentally prepare yourself to surrender to the instructions of the DJ. Even if you're the kind of guy who just doesn't dance, getting out on the floor is an essential part of the evening. Really, its okay. The worst thing that can happen is that you give your daughter something to tease you about. If you are instructed to put your right hip in and shake it all about, just do it. If a human locomotive chugs by, grab on. And please don't forget how to spell Y-M-C-A.

The evening will go by quickly. And so will the years. Pretty soon she'll be in middle school, way too mature for the organized "Daddy-Daughter Date Nite." When that happens, I recommend you create a revised, scaled-down version of the event for just you and your blossoming daughter. When the park-district brochure comes out, let the announcement serve as a reminder to make reservations for two at one of the nicer restaurants in town. Instead of doing the hokey-pokey, maybe the two of you can sit by candlelight and just talk. Talk about what's going on in her life. About girlfriends, hobbies, hopes and dreams. About boys and silly stuff that brothers and moms just don't get.

—————————— **Takeaway** ——————————

Got a little girl? Check with your local park district or ask some other dads you know about the nearest "Daddy-Daughter Date Nite." Put it on your calendar. Surrender yourself to the evening. Make it magical. (And look for the same kind of special events for your son as well.)

> *"The father of a daughter is nothing but a high-class hostage. A father turns a stony face to his sons, berates them, shakes his antlers, paws the ground, snorts, runs them off into the underbrush, but when his daughter puts her arm over his shoulder and says, 'Daddy, I need to ask you something,' he is a pat of butter in a hot frying pan."*
>
> —Garrison Keillor

39

Sons Need Their Dad...

To Be Their Sparring Partner

If a daughter needs to dance with her daddy, a son needs to do battle with him. As he prepares to make his mark in the world, a boy needs to take stock of his own abilities, measuring himself against the man who forever will be the prototype for what it means to be a husband, father, protector, and provider. That's you, Dad.

Doing battle with your son is not about breaking his spirit, butting heads maliciously, wielding your authority unfairly, or trampling his manhood. If that's where you're headed, exit that road quickly. Your job is to be a good sparring partner—figuratively and perhaps even literally.

Preparing for an upcoming bout, a boxer will spend hours in the practice ring with his sparring partner. Their goal is not to do physical harm to each other—instead it's to hone their skills, get into the best physical shape possible, and discover their own best strategies for victory. Does your son need to work on his jab, uppercut, or roundhouse? How is his footwork and blocking? Can he deliver a knockout punch? We can beat the metaphor to death, but suffice it to say, practice makes perfect. Because you care so much about your son, you are the ideal foil to help him determine his strengths and weaknesses while competing in a safe environment.

In the practice ring, sparring partners sometimes go half or three-quarter speed to allow their colleague to work on strategic moves. Both boxers are well-protected with headgear and extra padding. Both boxers grow in the process without risk. In the same way, a father can challenge his son in any physical or intellectual competition and both of you will gain wisdom and experience in the battle.

In early competitions, Dad should expect to emerge victorious. As the years pass, the goal is for the son to prevail more and more often.

Should a father ever reduce his effort to let his son win? My recommendation is no. Kids will know right away if you're not doing your best. When they do eventually earn an authentic victory over their old man, they'll never know for sure, and the significance will be lost. On the other hand, can a father manipulate circumstance so that a young warrior gets a taste of victory at an early age? Absolutely. Be clever. Be wise. Be humble and gracious in defeat.

Examples? In a one-on-one father-son basketball, let's say your middle-schooler is playing the game of his young life and the score is very close. On your next few jump shots, see if you can muster all your skills to bounce your shot off the back of the rim and into his waiting hands for the rebound. Afterward, shake his hand and let him enjoy his victory, perhaps tolerating just a bit of playful trash talk. Just make sure you dominate in the next few games. You don't want him to get too cocky.

In chess, if your son has been improving his skills by playing with peers, then maybe he has earned the right to taste victory against Dad. Don't ignore your favorite strategies, and certainly don't "accidentally" leave key pieces unprotected. Instead, simply don't use all the weapons in your arsenal, including those strategies you learned from that old Russian chess master, and see if your son rises to the challenge. In other words, go three-quarter speed and see if your son rises to the challenge. It takes real artistry to throw a game of chess (or checkers) without your opponent realizing it.

Pick a competition, any competition. Sooner than you may anticipate, they'll be beating your pants off. Then, because of your role as sparring partner, you can even take a small amount of credit for their improvement. Also, because you played a key role in their development it will be ever so much sweeter each time they claim victory against one of their peers.

For now, go ahead and dominate in Ping-Pong and Scrabble. It's to your son's advantage if you catch more fish, hit a straighter drive, or stack a higher house of cards. As long as you can outperform him, do it. It will give the young man something to shoot for and a reason to keep asking you to play. Just don't forget to celebrate when he passes you by.

By the way, none of this applies to video games. Not once will you beat him. Unless he lets you.

Takeaway

Got a little boy? Be the kind of competitor you want him to be. Tenacious. Spirited. Honest. Humble. Courageous. Willing to practice. Eager to learn. (Truth be told, all this goes for daughters as well.)

> *"I cheat my boys every chance I get. I trade with the boys and skin 'em and I just beat 'em every time I can. I want to make 'em sharp."*
> —JOHN D. ROCKEFELLER (1839–1937)

40

Kids Need Their Dad...

To Establish and Enforce Some Ironclad Family Rules

Rules are good things. Universal rules that apply to all people and all things establish order, provide security, and set boundaries within which people can flourish and grow without fear. *Do not kill. Do not lie. Do not steal.* The other seven of the Ten Commandments are also good examples. Traffic laws keep us safe. Truancy laws make sure kids get a minimum education. Spelling rules help us communicate.

Similarly, families can and should establish their own rules to keep anarchy at bay. So you know what I'm talking about, here are a few Payleitner family rules. Even though they have never been written down (until now), they are understood by every member of the family. I am not sure of the origin of most of these rules, but I confirm that they are unequivocally unbreakable. (Unless sometimes they are broken. Then it's every man for himself.)

- Mom goes through the mail first.

- All children will learn to juggle the summer after sixth grade.

- If one parent is in the car, the oldest child in the car rides shotgun. Except on extraordinary occasions.

- Baseball gloves and baseball caps for teams on which a family member is currently playing are sacred objects. They cannot be borrowed, stolen, or abused.

- If he is in the room, Max controls the remote.

- Within reason, it is permissible to throw anything to anyone at anytime and expect it to be caught without incident. That includes glassware, ketchup bottles, spatulas, remotes, card chairs, and tweezers. If the item falls to the ground, it is the fault of the catcher. It is assumed that the tosser will always make a quality toss. That's what Payleitners do.

- Siblings attend all concerts, athletic events, productions, and performances unless they have a really good excuse. In any case, no guilt trips are allowed.

- Peanut butter does not go in the fridge.

- Chili is made with kidney, not pinto, beans.

- Christmas morning, no presents are opened unless everyone is in the room, and then we open one present at a time.

- Once a photo is posted on the wall of shame, no family member can take it down. (Except Mom.)

- We grasp hands as a family around the table and one of us prays out loud before each meal. At restaurants, it's short and quiet.

- As we pray, guests are expected to participate.

- It's usually Dad who prays, but if Dad says your name and asks you to pray, you do.

- Now that we're older, everyone does their own laundry. Except Dad. (Although Mom certainly will do a load for you if you ask her nicely.)

- When you leave the house, tell someone or leave a note saying when you expect to return.

- The stapler in Dad's office inscribed "Dad Only" is to be used by Dad only. (Unless you really need it. But then you must bring it right back. Unless you forget.)

- Dad is the only person who can take out the recyclables. Obviously, it's way too mentally and physically challenging for anyone else.

Well, perhaps some of those Payleitner rules are bendable, but still you get the idea. What's the overarching purpose of family rules? None, really. Except that's what families naturally do. Mom, Dad, sons, and daughters learn to co-exist in ways unique to every family.

Your ironclad family rules are a celebration and proof that you're a family. The occasional breaking of those rules proves that life goes on.

Your assignment, Dad, is to think of a few of your own family rules and then next time you're together, share them with your kids and see how many other rules your family can think of. (Send them to me at www.fathers52 .com and I'll include them in my next book.)

Takeaway

Celebrate the uniqueness of your family. See the big picture. Babies are born, family members pass away, laughter echoes, tears are shed, but the legacy of family lives on.

"The family is one of Nature's masterpieces."
—George Santayana (1863–1952)

Kids Need Their Dad...

To Multitask

Just kidding. All the dads I know can do only one thing at a time. Multitasking is totally out of our league. So my suggestion is, don't even try. Instead, choose to do one thing at a time. And do it well.

Sometimes (usually) your best option is to go with the way God wired you. Besides, when a dad does one thing well, he can actually achieve multiple goals in the doing.

For example, throwing yourself 100 percent completely into reading a bedtime story to your eight-year-old daughter can simultaneously deliver more than a half-dozen benefits—long- and short-term. You're strengthening your relationship and making memories. You're conveying the importance of reading. You're creating a positive experience within the walls of her private space, which increases the chance you will be welcome there in the future under more difficult circumstances.

Depending on which book you choose, you may be teaching a lesson, sharing a learning experience, or gaining insight into your daughter's world. You're practicing the art of reading aloud for read-aloud opportunities you may have in the future at school, at church, or years from now with your grandchildren. Most importantly, you're setting the mood for a tucking-in prayer and a goodnight kiss.

All those things happen because you are focusing with laser-point intensity on the single all-important task of reading a bedtime story to your little girl. You aren't nagging about a few items of clothing on the floor. You aren't interrogating her about the new poster of the latest boy band and their ripped blue jeans and exposed abs. You aren't quizzing her about her homework.

You're just reading. If she happens to bring up some of those other issues, that's fine. But sometimes, the fewer items on your agenda, the better.

So Dad, don't feel guilty if you can't multitask. Instead, celebrate your ability to focus on one thing with complete concentration and single-minded intensity. Even if it's just grilling pork chops, installing a garbage disposal, changing a diaper, or watching football. You are the master of your moment.

Actually, Dad, the best part of doing one thing at a time might be that suddenly other members of the family are forced to take on a little personal responsibility around the home. When you're in the middle of doing what you're doing, they are forced to figure out how to subdue the obstinate grass trimmer all by themselves. They tackle the challenge of an overflowing wastebasket. They learn that a lightbulb won't change itself. They figure out how to get the bicycle chain back on the gears without you. If any of these jobs prove too formidable, you're still available, but isn't it nice to see the kids taking initiative on their own? Maybe that's why God chose to not give men the gift of multitasking.

By the way, this chapter was inspired by my wife, Rita, who can simultaneously knit, cook dinner, watch TV, entertain the dog, pray for a college-age son traveling cross-country, do laundry, respond to urgent PTO business, tell me about her day, balance the checkbook, and somehow also help me stay focused on the one thing I'm trying to do at that moment.

Takeaway

Know your limits. When you can't do it all, take comfort that your family members have all kinds of gifts and abilities waiting to be discovered and put to good use. That's how families work best.

"The successful warrior is the average man, with laser-like focus."
—BRUCE LEE (1940–1973)

Kids Need Their Dad...

To Take the Lead on Halloween

Near the end of October, Christian parents fall into three camps. Some casually say, "Trick or treat, pumpkin carving, and silly costumes? It's harmless fun." A second group counters, "Don't be fooled. Halloween and everything it stands for opens the door—literally—to Satan." Most of us fall into the third group. We want to protect our kids from all things sinister, but we don't want them to miss out on the joys of being a kid.

Let's start with some indisputable facts. First, *Halloween has some nasty roots*. The Druids were the original New Age high priests. Every October 31, on the eve of their new year, the Druids led the ancient Celts in a rousing tribute to Samhain, the Lord of the Dead. Their form of trick-or-treating was, to say the least, ghoulish and deadly. As it was originally celebrated, Halloween was Satan's High Holiday.

Another indisputable fact about Halloween is that *kids love it*. They dress up, get free candy, and stay up late, and Mom and Dad let them get away with stuff they normally wouldn't. Next to Christmas, it's the ultimate kids' holiday.

Plus, it's inescapable. The stores are filled with Halloween displays. All October long, in every neighborhood and schoolyard, kids talk about their costumes. In the days to follow, they brag about how many houses they visited and the loot they collected. What parents want to be "the bad guys" by depriving their children of such a fun-filled, community-wide event? Of course, just because it's everywhere, doesn't make it right. As a matter of fact, in our postmodern world, any social trend that is expanding should be cause for suspicion for careful parents.

So how can a Christian dad reconcile these conflicting views of Halloween?

One courageous plan of action is to ban any celebration of Halloween from your home. I know parents who have taken this route and I respect them. I applaud them. I'm a little envious of their firm convictions. They have taken to heart Romans 12:1-2, which gives us the clear instruction, "Do not conform any longer to the pattern of this world, but be transformed by the renewing of your mind."

Many families and churches replace Halloween with a Harvest Festival or celebration of All Saints' Day that may include costumes and pumpkin carving. I honor the decision and faithfulness of those loving parents.

My recommendation is not to ignore Halloween, but to be proactive. Fighting fire with fire. Use October 31 as a day to combat the Father of Lies. Our battle plan could actually be modeled after how secularists have attacked Christmas. Have you noticed how hardcore pagans still celebrate the December holiday? They simply leave Christ out of it. What's more, they insist that any mention of Christ be banished to behind church doors. Annual lawsuits insist that cashiers and bell ringers refrain from saying "Merry Christmas" and that nativity scenes not be visible from public venues. Advancing their tactics further, they mock and belittle anyone who attempts to honor the real meaning of Christmas.

Putting your opponents on the defensive is a pretty clever strategy. So let's take a page from that playbook. A thoughtful editorial in *Christianity Today* by Anderson M. Rearick III suggests we reclaim Halloween by openly laughing at Satan.

> Should the forces of evil be mocked? Should Satan be laughed at? He most certainly should be. At the beginning of *The Screwtape Letters*, C.S. Lewis includes two telling quotations, the first from Martin Luther: "The best way to drive out the devil, if he will not yield to texts of Scripture, is to jeer and flout him, for he cannot bear scorn." The second comes from Thomas More: "The devil... the proud spirit cannot endure to be mocked."
>
> The one thing Satan cannot bear, these great men believe, is to be an object of laughter. His pride is undermined by his own knowledge that his infernal rebellion against God is in reality an absurd farce. Hating laughter, he demands to be taken seriously. Indeed, I would say that those Christians who spend the night of October

31 filled with concern over what evils might be (and sometimes are) taking place are doing the very thing Lucifer wants them to do. By giving him this respect, such believers are giving his authority credence.[9]

As dads, we can further frustrate Satan by arming our children for the spiritual battle. Inform your kids about the history of Halloween. Warn them that Satan and spiritual warfare are very real. Explain to your children the dangers of opening the door—even a tiny bit—for the Father of Lies. You can even take Halloween traditions and turn each negative into a positive. Your local Christian bookstore has colorful Halloween tracts which you can buy in quantity and tuck into the bags of trick-or-treaters. Encourage costumes that have positive meanings. Several years ago, my son Alec wore a number 55 Dodgers uniform—for the Christian pitcher Orel Hershiser.

Since we know Satan hates happy families, let's also use his day to make ours stronger. Tromp through pumpkin patches together. Slice up a defenseless pumpkin. Walk the kids around the neighborhood reminding them to say, "Thank you." Teach them to share their goodies. (Maybe with you!)

Finally, pray. Pray with your kids several times throughout the day. Pray ahead of time with your Bible study or men's group. Pray for the physical and spiritual safety of all the children in your neighborhood. When you call on the name "Jesus," know that Satan has already been defeated.

Takeaway

Just to be clear. Halloween is not to be taken lightly. It's recruitment time for witches, cults, and Satanists. Stay vigilant against occult activity within your circle of influence. Understand that if we confront Satan on our own, we will lose.

> *"Our struggle is not against flesh and blood, but against the rulers, against the authorities, against the powers of this dark world and against the spiritual forces of evil in the heavenly realms."*
> —EPHESIANS 6:12

Kids Need Their Dad...

To Anticipate Their Every Need

That sounds terrible, doesn't it? "Anticipating their every need" sounds like you have lowered yourself to the position of servant ready to wait on your child hand and foot, responding instantly to their every whim. Actually, what I'm talking about is just the opposite. Anticipating your children's needs actually makes your life easier.

I call it "anticipatory parenting." The goal is to be so aware of your kids' needs that you know what they need before they need it.

A few examples may help. Have a fresh diaper and several baby wipes ready BEFORE you open the dirty diaper. Plug up the electrical outlets BEFORE your toddler starts crawling. Check out the schools BEFORE you move into a new neighborhood.

Make sense? Sure it does. But it's not always easy. To stay one step ahead of your kids, you need to spend time with them, know where they're headed, and know what's going on in their sweet little heads.

Anticipatory parenting is not just about preventing disasters. It can also help you be a hero in the eyes of your child. Play catch with your kids BEFORE baseball tryouts and they have a better chance of making the team. Have a stash of markers and poster boards in your closet BEFORE they come to you Sunday night at 7 p.m. frantic about a project due the next day. Put their birthdays, concerts, and game schedules on your calendar BEFORE any other appointments and you'll be in attendance at most of them.

The importance of anticipatory parenting becomes even more obvious as the kids get older.

Have your young teenagers commit to sexual purity BEFORE their first date. If you wait until their friends are already sexually active, it's way too late. The phrase "Just Say No" to drugs may seem a little corny, but it's your job to help your kids find ways to say no BEFORE they are confronted with that decision.

Make sure they understand the concept of defensive driving BEFORE they get their license. As they sit in the passenger seat and scan the road for potholes, brake lights, kids running out from between parked cars, and bonehead drivers, they're actually learning anticipatory driving.

As they enter the job force, you can help them know what to expect in job interviews and what employers expect from new hires. Because you know their gifts and abilities, you can even help them choose a college major or career path in which they will succeed BEFORE they even get their first paycheck.

The most quoted Bible verse on parenting is really all about anticipatory parenting. "Train a child in the way he should go, and when he is old he will not turn from it" (Proverbs 22:6).

Of course, children make their own choices, and parents shouldn't hold themselves responsible every time their kids mess up. But ask any parent with a child who flunked out, tuned out, or got into a ton of trouble. Those parents will almost always say, "I didn't see it coming."*

The most critical instance of anticipatory planning is one that faces all of us, not just our kids. It's knowing where we are going to spend eternity BEFORE we close out our time here on earth. Heaven is waiting for those who trust Jesus Christ. Because that's a legitimate concern that can keep a dad up at night, I suggest you take care of business ASAP. First, get your own head and heart right with God. Understand your need for a Savior, confess your sins, and ask him into your life as counselor and king. Then lead your kids in that same prayer. Suddenly, your family's citizenship in heaven is secure and your biggest worries in life are over.

Jesus tells us,

> Do not let your hearts be troubled. Trust in God; trust also in me.
> In my Father's house are many rooms; if it were not so, I would

---

* The foregoing material in this chapter is adapted from Jay Payleitner, *40 Days to Your Best Life for Men* (Colorado Springs: Honor Books, 2002), 101-103. ©2002 Cook Communications Ministries. *40 Days to Your Best Life For Men* by Honor Books. Used with permission. May not be further reproduced. All rights reserved.

have told you. I am going there to prepare a place for you. And if I go and prepare a place for you, I will come back and take you to be with me that you also may be where I am (John 14:1-3).

The driving force behind anticipatory parenting is that you are setting your kids up for success. Don't let the busyness of today distract you from having long-term visions for your children.

Takeaway

Picture your kids at school tomorrow. Or on some other field of battle. Envision them attending college, launching a career, or starting a family. What can you do today to help them succeed tomorrow?

> *"An ounce of prevention is worth a pound of cure."*
> —Benjamin Franklin (1706–1790)

#44

Kids Need Their Dad...

To Spin a Bucket Overhead

Eventually, every kid will learn to multiply. It usually happens late in second grade. They will also learn about "opposites." That's basic kindergarten curriculum. In fourth grade, most school districts teach centrifugal force. In middle school, kids will learn how to bisect an angle with a compass and a straight edge. Your school district should be able to tell you exactly what they teach and when.

When a teacher introduces new concepts to a class full of kids, three things happen. One, it's immediately considered *work*. There's no choice involved, and students have to put effort into learning these new ideas. A good teacher may be able to make it interesting, but it's still work that needs to be done. Second, some kids pick up on the concept faster than others. My wife often reminds me that not everything is a competition, but wouldn't you prefer your own kid to be in the winner's bracket when it comes to new topics in the classroom? Third, kids start making instant judgments concerning their classmates. "He's smart." "He's so dumb." You can't fight it—that's just the way it is. But again, shouldn't we be setting our kids up for achievement?

Here's an idea. Not the week before. Not the semester before. But *years* before, go ahead and teach a few of these concepts to your kids. Make it a game!

Do you know a three-year-old? Ask them, "What's the opposite of *up*?" They won't know. Tell them with great sincerity, "The opposite of up is *down*!" Then ask them, "What is the opposite of *cold*?" They won't know. Tell them the "The opposite of cold is *hot*!" Do the same with big/little, loud/quiet,

155

slow/fast, closed/open, nice/mean, clean/dirty, yes/no, off/on, and so on. Use your best vocal expressiveness, use your hands, look in their face, mime the answer as you say it. After four or five examples, suddenly their little face lights up and they understand! It's amazing. It's a rush for them and for you. In a couple years, when the kindergarten teacher starts teaching "opposites," your kid is going to be top of the class. Suddenly, they will be earmarked as a bright student worthy of special attention for the rest of their school career. This is strategic fathering. Going into kindergarten, all the moms have already made sure their kids know colors, ABCs, and two plus two. But only your kid will know "opposites." The best part is that you taught them!

Do the same with multiplication when your kid is in first grade. But don't ask, "What is five times two?" That sounds confusing. That's work. Instead, ask "What is five, two times?" Use your hands as demonstration. Then ask, "What is four, two times?" Then ask, "What is four, three times!" A sharp first-grader (your kid) will get it. Be warned, you've turned learning into a game and they may never want to stop. That's when you know you have put them way ahead of the curve.

One more example. On the next nice day, invite your second-grader out to your driveway to wash your car. Ask them if they think you can hold the bucket of water upside down over your head without spilling it. They will laugh and say, "No way, Daddy!" Then spin that bucket over your head without losing a drop. They'll be amazed, and you will have demonstrated centrifugal and centripetal force. (Look it up, if you don't remember.)

You can see how this concept is really an extension of "anticipatory parenting." But there's an edge to it, a little subterfuge. Dad, you're running a bit of a con game. Your kid may or may not actually be any smarter than the other kids. Still, everyone in that classroom has new, heightened expectations for your child's performance.

Funny thing about expectations. They tend to come true.

Takeaway

Kids love to learn stuff from Dad. Take full advantage. Especially when they're young.

"If you think you can, you can. And if you
think you can't, you're right."
—HENRY FORD (1863–1947)

Kids Need Their Dad...

To Be Ichthyusiastic

That's not a real word. A friend of mine and former pastor, Rich French, made it up, and I think it accurately expresses some of the most important things kids need from their dads.

What would it mean to be an "ichthyusiastic" dad? Because it's not a real word (yet), I'm going to just go ahead and make up my own definition. An ichthyusiastic dad is a Christian who has a firm grasp on his purpose, his source of hope, and his place in this world—and isn't afraid to exhibit that confidence to his kids and others in his sphere of influence.

The *ichthys*, as you may know, is the elegantly simple fish insignia that in the last generation has become widely seen on the rear bumpers and trunk lids of cars owned by well-intentioned believers. (Recent sacrilegious and contentious versions of the ichthys have robbed the original symbol of its primal meaning. And they tick me off.)

The fish symbol first appeared in the catacombs beneath Rome, underground cemeteries used as refuges by early Christians. Nearly 600 miles of winding caverns still exist today. Two-thousand-year-old carvings in the catacombs reflect a kind of hope not found in cemeteries above ground. Pagan headstones might be inscribed with the words "Live for the present hour, since we are sure of nothing else." But down in the catacombs you can still see carvings of the Good Shepherd, crowns, vines, and the ichthys fish. Inscriptions read, "The Word of God is not bound" and "Victorious in peace and Christ!"

In the first century, persecuted Christians would gather below ground for prayer, worship, and fellowship. Above ground, the ichthys became a way to identify and communicate in secret with other believers.

These early believers are pretty good role models for today's faith-filled fathers. They know their hope is in Christ. They meet regularly for prayer and worship. They lift each other up with encouraging words and regular fellowship. They are well aware that they are living countercultural to the ways of the world.

How can you tell an ichthyusiastic dad? He may very well have a metallic fish symbol on the back of his car, but more importantly his life demonstrates evidence that he is a man of God. For example:

An ichthyusiastic dad isn't afraid to express love.

> By this all men will know that you are my disciples, if you love one another (John 13:35).

An ichthyusiastic dad carries himself with a confidence that comes from knowing he is pursuing God's will in his life, and when he falls short, his constant communication with the Creator of the universe will help him get back on track.

> This is the confidence we have in approaching God: that if we ask anything according to his will, he hears us (1 John 5:14).

An ichthyusiastic dad may actually take a little grief on the job or in the neighborhood for not going along with the crowd. He doesn't go all-night bar crawling. He excuses himself when the pornography gets passed around or the cursing escalates. He doesn't take home company supplies or pad his expense account. He recognizes that his life stands opposed to the expectations of today's culture. If he is judged or ridiculed for standing on a principle, that's a good thing.

> If you suffer as a Christian, do not be ashamed, but praise God that you bear that name (1 Peter 4:16).

An ichthyusiastic dad knows that this world is not his home. That no matter what happens in this life—for good or bad—something better awaits him in the next life.

> We are citizens of heaven, where the Lord Jesus Christ lives. And we are eagerly waiting for him to return as our Savior (Philippians 3:20 NLT).

An ichthyusiastic dad isn't perfect, but he lives with an integrity so that the rest of the world doesn't view him as a hypocrite. He knows his kids are watching too.

> Be careful to live properly among your unbelieving neighbors. Then even if they accuse you of doing wrong, they will see your honorable behaviors, and they will give honor to God when he judges the world (1 Peter 2:12 NLT).

An icthyusiastic dad hangs out with other dads. But not to escape his family or keep the stools warm at the local sports bar. He has a small group of men who all want to be good fathers; they meet regularly to study Scripture, dig through books (like this one), and pray for each other. Knowing they can't do it on their own, they get guidance from their church leadership or quality organizations like the guys at The National Center for Fathering (www.fathers.com). They make each other stronger and wiser.

> As iron sharpens iron, so one man sharpens another (Proverbs 27:17).

An ichthyusiastic dad doesn't have to spend annual sabbaticals in a monastery, preach on the street corners, or travel on year-long mission trips to undeveloped countries. But he does spend regular time in God's Word, humbly share his faith with family and friends, and look for opportunities to leave his comfort zone to help those in need.

That kind of enthusiasm (or ichthyusiasm) has a surprising appeal to the next generation. It actually draws your kids toward you. It helps them see the gospel in action. A sincere, humble, well-equipped faith is exactly what your kids want for themselves. If they see it in you, Dad, you've just found yourself a partner in building God's kingdom.

For the record, I don't have a fish on my car. Partly because I'm not sure I can live up to the standards of what it should mean to be a Christian. I know Christians don't need to be perfect, but I am a little afraid of cutting someone off in traffic and thereby damaging the reputation of those who profess Christ. That's something I need to keep working on.

Takeaway

When it comes to passing your faith on to your children, who you are is much more important than what you say. They are watching. And they see it all.

> *"I believe that what we become depends on what our fathers teach us at odd moments, when they aren't trying to teach us."*
> —UMBERTO ECO (1932–)

Kids Need Their Dad...

To Quit Golf

I totally recommend coaching your sons' and daughters' sports teams when they're eight years old or so. Even if you never really played that particular sport, you still know more than they do. As they approach their teenage years, kids begin to think they know more than their dads, and they may be right. But for a few years at least you can enjoy quite a few benefits from being their dad and their coach.

For one thing, it's scheduled time with your kid both on the field and in the car. It also gives you a chance to observe them as they interact with their peers and to assess their giftedness in the areas of athletic ability, coachability, perseverance, and leadership. When you coach your kids' teams, you automatically have something to talk about through the highs and lows of the season. Those conversations may include setting personal goals, game-day strategies, analyzing the strengths and weaknesses of teammates, and even asking your son or daughter for advice on how you can be a better coach.

For all five of my kids, I made sure to coach them during the summer after third and fourth grade. During those ten seasons, I taught dozens of kids from my hometown how to "not throw like a girl," "use your glove like a dustpan," "squash the bug," and "run through first base." Some got it, some didn't. Some went on to play college ball years later, and they've been fun to follow. Some played their last season of baseball or softball for Coach Payleitner, and that's okay. All of them had moments of failure and success. All of them learned to better appreciate the beauty of baseball, and they got a few life lessons thrown in at no extra charge.

I learned a lesson or two myself.

I remember one pretty good little ballplayer who showed up faithfully every practice and every game. His mom always brought a book and would look up from her reading occasionally to see the action. His dad could never come to any games. We played during the week, and apparently the dad traveled Monday through Friday. Because of a rainout, we had a game rescheduled for a Saturday, and this little guy was all excited because now he could finally show off for his father. I remember him saying, "My dad can come to the game!" and I made a mental note to start him at short-stop. On Saturday, the young man came to the field hanging his head. I asked what was going on and he told me his dad couldn't come because... he had...to play golf.

The kid was crushed. I was angry. And that dad didn't have a clue.

Truthfully, I don't know the entire situation. I never met that father. I don't know what responsibilities or burdens he was facing. I don't know about the relationship he had with his wife or any other kids. But I do know he missed out. It was a morning in July like so many other mornings. It came and went. An opportunity lost. A father-son moment that never happened.

Okay, maybe I shouldn't be blaming golf for this father's poor decision. But since then, I confess to making an instant judgment every time I hear a guy boast about his terrific weekend playing 18 or 36 holes. It's not fair, I know, but I get a mental image of his son at home alone bouncing a tennis ball off the garage door. Without all the facts, it isn't fair to judge the commitment any man has to his family. But I can't help myself.

Do all kids really need their dad to quit golf? Probably not. But on the other hand, Dad, if you are regularly choosing golf (or any sport or hobby) over time with your children, then yes—quit. Put your clubs in storage. Cancel your tee times for the summer. Walk in the front door, announce, "I'm quitting golf to spend more time with my family!" and listen to the cheers.

Of course, there is room for a completely different perspective on the topic, and maybe you're already living that dream. If your kids are getting older and you walk the fairways alongside them a dozen times each summer, then you should disregard this chapter. If they outdrive you and win their share of holes, that's even better. Then I'm not judging, I'm jealous. My new recommendation would be to keep that tradition going as long as you can. Golf (or whatever your passion is) can be a wonderful tool that brings the generations together.

Takeaway

There are moments in every kid's life when he needs his dad. Unfortunately, a father can never know when that moment comes. The only choice—the best choice—is to be there every chance you get. Even if that means rearranging your schedule, passing up a promotion, or putting one of your passions on hold.

"It is easier to build strong children than to repair broken men."
—FREDERICK DOUGLASS (1818–1895)

To Kiss His Wife in the Kitchen

At least three things happen when you kiss your wife in the kitchen. First, you're telling your bride that you love her.

Second, you're telling your kids that you love their mom.

Third, you're demonstrating to your kids that passion can happen in a committed, lifelong marriage relationship. Most of the kisses they see on television or the movies are couples who aren't married (at least to each other). Hollywood writers and producers seem to think that once a couple is married, sexuality becomes less than interesting. After the wedding, the romance is gone, so to speak. Well, I disagree. And so does God.

> A man will leave his father and mother and be united to his wife, and they will become one flesh (Genesis 2:24).

> Marriage should be honored by all, and the marriage bed kept pure (Hebrews 13:4).

> Enjoy life with your wife, whom you love (Ecclesiastes 9:9).

> May you rejoice in the wife of your youth...may her breasts satisfy you always, may you ever be captivated by her love (Proverbs 5:18-19).

Through words and actions, you need to let your kids know that you and your wife have fully committed yourself to God's view of marriage. An embrace and five-second kiss in the busiest room in the house in broad daylight is strong evidence that you have become one flesh spiritually, emotionally, physically, eternally.

Someone once said, "The best thing a father can do for his kids is love their mother." In other words, children need Dad to establish a solid family foundation from which they can launch themselves into the world. You may have heard the argument that a young person who enjoys a secure and comfortable life at home may never want to leave. Just the opposite. If you provide a safe harbor, your maturing children will be strengthened, emboldened, and ready for full deployment. They will want to experience what Mom and Dad have. I believe much of today's cynicism, bitterness, and anger comes from family backgrounds in disarray.

Marriage is a gift designed by God. It's a gift between a husband and wife. And it's a gift of love modeled to children by their parents.

An illustration I saw presented by a speaker years ago helped me tremendously to visualize where God should be in my marriage. Imagine a triangle with God at the top and a husband and wife at the two bottom corners. The closer the man and woman get to God, the closer they are to each other.

A 2008 study by the Center for Marriage and Families concluded that couples 18 to 55 who attend church several times a month report happier marriages than those who rarely or never attend.[10] No surprise there. The better you know the Designer, the more you appreciate His work.

Want to know real intimacy with your bride? Pray together on a regular basis. Often youth pastors will counsel high-school couples who are committed to following Christ...to NOT pray together. Prayer is such an intimate act that it often leads to physical and emotional bonding, something those young unmarried couples are trying to avoid.

In summary, the formula for a great marriage? Pray. Kiss.

By the way, a fourth thing might happen when a husband and wife kiss in the kitchen. Their third-grader (especially a son) might go, "Ewwww!" or their teenager might wisecrack, "Get a room!" Dad, that's a sure signal you're doing it right.

--- **Takeaway** ---

You have to feel sorry for couples who don't understand the spiritual side of sexual intimacy. They're missing out. Like everything else, sex is a gift from God to be opened at just the right time. Make sure your kids know that.

"There is no more lovely, friendly, and charming relationship,
communion, or company than a good marriage."
—MARTIN LUTHER (1483–1546)

48

Kids Need Their Dad...

To Respect Their Mom

I have a fantastic wife. Rita and I just passed 30 years of delightful wedded bliss. In many ways our life together just keeps getting better and better. Till death do us part. She's beautiful and intelligent; she's the best mom in the world and she makes me a better man. If it weren't for Rita, I would likely be living in a van down by the river. She's easy to love and has earned my respect and admiration.

Honestly, I don't know what it's like to be in long-term conflict with my wife. I don't know what it's like to be antagonistic or adversarial. I don't know what it's like to be separated or divorced, wondering what happened to my storybook life, scraping up child support, and agonizing over not being allowed to see my kids. If that describes your life, then my heart aches for you and your entire family.

Marriages are tossed aside too easily in our disposable society. But there's help available. Entire libraries and professions are dedicated to saving marriages and rescuing families. This short chapter cannot possibly be much more than a simple reminder and short assignment for dads.

The reminder is this: No matter what, your kids need you to respect their mom. Treat her with dignity. Refrain from shouting, blaming, or name-calling. Respond to her requests, keep the lines of communication open, and work things out in a way that is as fair as possible to all parties involved.

That's not just in divorce proceedings. Respect, common courtesy, and communication are the bare minimum for all husbands to provide for the woman with whom they once exchanged wedding vows. If those three elements are present, then even estranged couples still have a chance to start looking past differences, focus on the positives, and rekindle the love that brought you together in the first place. It begins with respect.

The assignment then is this: Put yourself in your children's shoes. It doesn't matter how old they are. When parents are in conflict, their offspring all endure a similar range of emotions. Guilt. Fear. Confusion. Anger. Torn allegiances. Grief. Shame. Sadness. Loneliness. Anxiety.

What's a dad to do? Once you begin to empathize with what your kids may be going through, then move toward making things right. That may include an apology from you and a willingness to wait patiently for their forgiveness. It also may include a move toward reconciliation with your wife. But again, that's not the point of this short chapter.

The previous chapter said, "Kiss your wife in the kitchen." I stand by that advice. The effort it takes to build a marriage is a lot easier than to rebuild a broken one. It's also a lot easier to walk down the hallway to kiss your kids goodnight than to drive across town and pick them up for your weekly visitation.

Takeaway

A word to husbands who are committed to their wives and may have breezed through this short chapter without much concern: Ask your bride how you are doing in the area of showing respect, listening to her opinions, and heeding her advice. Then respect, listen, and heed her words.

"A wife of noble character who can find?
She is worth far more than rubies.
Her husband has full confidence in her
and lacks nothing of value.
She brings him good, not harm,
all the days of her life."
—PROVERBS 31:10-12

49

Kids Need Their Dad...

To Set the Bar Pretty High

After Rae Anne was named all-conference catcher her sophomore year in high school and was leading the conference in home runs, I made a mistake. I began to *expect* an extra base hit every time she came to the plate. It got to the point that I was disappointed with a single. No pressure there, right? Later in the season, after she went without a hit for a couple games in a tournament, I came to a conclusion that it's really okay for my gifted daughter to have an occasional bad day or even a little bit of a slump. But then in her last plate appearance of the day she crushed a home run that shattered a windshield in the parking lot. And my expectations rose even higher, if that's possible.

I certainly will not take any credit for Rae Anne's blast that day, but it did get me thinking about the idea of "expectations." Setting goals is one thing. You might make them, you might not. Goals are something you work toward and hope for. On the other hand, expectations take performance to an entirely different level. An expectation isn't an option. Whatever it takes, it better happen.

A father's expectations are powerful tools. Mostly because they work without too many words. Establish a standard of performance and then expect your child to get the job done.

In athletics, setting goals for your kids is probably wiser than setting expectations. It can be oppressive to say to your son or daughter, "You will win so many matches" or, "You will set this school record." There are just too many factors that are out of your control. However, you can set expectations based on activity, not performance. For example: You are expected to show up on time ready for practice. You are expected to shoot 50 free throws before you go home. You are expected to improve on your "personal best" as the season progresses.

My son Max is a paragon of setting and meeting expectations. A single sheet of printer paper is still tacked on his bedroom wall inscribed with the words, "JANUARY 18—GET IT DONE." Back in 2002, Max had blown out his knee in a varsity football game. The surgeon hoped that, with intensive therapy, the knee might be ready for the spring baseball season in six months or so. Max attacked rehab with high expectations, and beginning January 12 he won 14 straight wrestling matches to earn a conference championship, regional championship, and a trip to the state finals. For Max, that date was more than a goal—it was an expectation.

Expectations aren't just limited to athletics. In fifth grade, Randy's teacher set 5000 pages as the standard to get an "A" in reading for the semester. Randy took that goal and set a new personal expectation. That year he read more than 10,000 pages of all kinds of novels and nonfiction, and perhaps that's part of the reason he's an acquisitions editor at Moody Publishing today.

Isaac, being the fourth son, faced all kinds of expectations and comparisons with his older brothers. For sure, he followed in their footsteps, but also blazed his own unique trails exploring interests beyond what he had seen his brothers achieve, including painting, CAD, rock climbing, and high-school soccer.

Expectations can also backfire on you. After our eldest, Alec, excelled at the piano at an early age, we just assumed all his siblings would do the same. Not so. Rita and I learned to change our expectations.

Applying this idea to our day-to-day lives, we can quickly rattle off a long list of expectations you might want to adapt for your children. Choose those which make sense for your family. And add your own.

Expect your kids to refrain from smoking.

Expect your kids to turn the lights out when they leave a room.

Expect your kids to hang up their clothes.

Expect cereal bowls in the dishwasher.

Expect soda cans in the recyclables.

Expect your kids to replace the toilet paper.

Expect your kids to wipe their feet when they come inside.

Expect them to ask before inviting a friend over.

Expect your kids to write thank-you notes.

Expect your kids to write down phone messages.

Expect your kids to wear their seat belts.

Expect your kids to brush their teeth twice a day.

Expect a phone call when they arrive at a distant destination.

Expect your kids to tell you where they're going when they leave the house.

Expect your kids to get up for church on Sunday morning.

Expect your kids to graduate high school.

Expect your kids to graduate college.

Expect perfect grandkids sometime in the future.

Some of this is common courtesy. Some is basic hygiene. Some is simple economics. All of it is groundwork for a successful life.

Kids need to know what is expected of them. And they need occasional gentle reminders of those expectations. What they don't need is nagging, whining, guilt trips, daily ultimatums, and aggravated parents. Set reasonable expectations early and often—by example or mandate—and watch them respond with enthusiasm.

Takeaway

Kids want to know your expectations. They want to delight you. That may not be as evident as they grow older, but that desire is still there.

"The greater danger for most of us lies not in setting
our aim too high and falling short; but in setting
our aim too low, and achieving our mark."
—MICHELANGELO (1475–1564)

50

Kids Need Their Dad...

To Wake Them Up for a Lunar Eclipse

L et's say the kids are all sound asleep in their rooms and you're watching the late news. The weather dude or dudette comes on and shows an image of the moon, which at that moment is half-covered by the shadow of the earth. What's your reaction? Your children's mother may disagree, but I say wake 'em up. Especially if they're in second or third grade. Children that age love making new discoveries and having the inside scoop on what happens after dark.

Shuffle them over to the window or drag them out onto the front lawn so they can see for themselves what happens when the sun, earth, and moon line up in a straight line. Just to clarify, this is not the monthly lunar cycle during which you see new moons, quarter moons, half moons, and full moons. A lunar eclipse is a relatively rare occurrence when the earth sneaks exactly between the sun and the moon, casting an obvious shadow on the surface of the moon. There's even a scientific term for the alignment of three celestial bodies. It's syzygy (pronounced *SIH-zih-jee*).

How often does this happen to the sun, earth, and moon? You could be proactive and look on the NASA Web site to view a calendar of partial or total lunar eclipses for the next several years. The frequency varies, and it may be a couple years between total eclipses viewable from North America. But like most extraordinary natural phenomena, if you watch the news or read the newspaper, you'll know what's going on and be able to share it with the kids.

What other stuff should a dad make it a point to point out to his kids?

If you see a full 180° rainbow, that's worth a second look with your crew. Take the time to debate the pros and cons of attempting to locate the pot of gold at each end and then explain the concept of refraction. Raindrops in the air act as tiny prisms. White sunlight enters one side of each drop and is refracted (or bent) at different angles depending on the wavelengths of light. The angle between the incoming ray and outgoing ray is different for each color. Red is 42°, violet is 40°, and so on. The circular rim created in the sky becomes a rainbow. You may even want to pull out your Bible and read from Genesis chapter 9, which records how rainbows were created as a gift from God reminding us of his promise that he would never again destroy all living things with a flood.

Even rarer is the double rainbow. Several years ago, a spectacular double rainbow inspired me to knock on doors up and down the street so the neighbor kids could also see God's multicolored display.

If you're out raking autumn leaves with the kids, make sure you point out any geese that fly over traveling north. Their V-formations are called echelons (pronounced *EH-shuh-lons*). You can ask your kids why they fly that way, but it's okay if they don't know. Even ornithologists disagree, offering two possible explanations. One is that the geese conserve energy by taking advantage of the upwash vortex fields created by the wings of the bird in front. The other possible explanation is that the V-angle facilitates orientation and communication among the flock. In any case, chatting about geese is a good excuse for taking a rake break.

There are also conflicting theories why fireflies light up. Scientists call it bioluminescence, and they know it's a chemical reaction inside the little bug bodies. Unlike a lightbulb, which produces heat, a firefly's light is "cold light," otherwise the fireflies' behinds would burn up. Kids enjoy that concept. There are several theories about why lightning bugs light up. The flashing may serve as a warning display to predators. Their bodies produce a steroid that makes them taste bad, and their light-emitting abdomen signals hungry birds to dine elsewhere. The flash patterns of adult fireflies probably also serve as a way to attract members of the opposite sex. That's an entirely different conversation to have with your kids.

Had enough science for today? Me too. There's no extra charge for all that stuff about syzygies, refraction, echelons, and bioluminescence. But here's the point. When your kids are little, you know more than them. That doesn't last forever, but the longer you can keep that illusion going, the better. By intentionally whipping out a few impressive scientific facts (or math concepts, historical perspectives, Bible truths, geographical gems, and so on) you will become the go-to guy for answers to your children's most difficult questions. Dad, that's a role you want to embrace and use to your long-term advantage. It may keep you on your toes, but it will also keep you inside the inner circle of your children's lives.

Takeaway

You want your kids to grow up to be smarter, wiser, better educated, better looking, and more successful than you. One way to increase the odds of that happening is to establish yourself as an unspoken benchmark for them to pass.

> *"When I was a boy of 14, my father was so ignorant I could hardly stand to have the old man around. But when I got to be 21, I was astonished at how much the old man had learned in seven years."*
>
> MARK TWAIN (1835–1910)

#51

Kids Need Their Dad...

To Equip Them
for Life Without You

Every generation of education experts seems to come up with their own version of classes that teach "decision-making skills." It might be "Quest" or "D.A.R.E." or "Skills for Life" or one of dozens of other much-heralded programs. With the best of intentions, your local school district introduces this nationally accredited miracle curriculum, presenting it as an exciting new way to fight gangs, drug abuse, teenage pregnancy, suicide, graffiti, and bullying. Suddenly all the young people in town are going to get along, make more friends, be financially independent, help little old ladies across the street, and keep their shirts tucked in.

Why do I sound so cynical? Because these programs cannot and will never point to an absolute truth. The best they have to offer are platitudes about "visualizing excellence" or choosing positive attitudes. Allegedly, they challenge boys and girls to be the best they can be. But what are the standards? Some of these curricula are filled with quotes and endorsements from athletes, actors, media personalities, and politicians. Apparently, just because you're on television means you know how to make wise decisions. Of course, these programs cannot point to God or hold up a Bible and say, "This is the standard." They can't even mention the Ten Commandments lest the ACLU swoop in and threaten a lawsuit based on the separation of church and state.

The best advice any of these programs can offer our young people is "search your heart and do what you think is best." Yikes! I don't think I want to live in a world in which teenagers are encouraged to follow their own whims and desires.

I feel bad now for trashing teachers and school boards; in many cases their hands are tied. I also know that many young people do not have a supportive father they can turn to for guidance and counsel, so it's possible these programs actually do have a positive impact for some. But your kids do have a dad who cares. You. One of your most important jobs is to do everything those "life skills programs" claim to be doing.

How can you do any better? The difference is that you can actually point out the characteristics of God and draw life skill principles from his example. God is love, so you can teach your children that love is the greatest commandment. God is life, so we know life is precious. God is truth, so we value honesty and integrity. God is creator, so we should nurture our own creative gifts. God is just, so we can trust him with our lives. God is infinite, so we must keep our eyes focused on eternity.

We can also point our children to Jesus as Savior. When it comes to "decision-making skills," the one decision to follow Christ is the most important choice your son or daughter will ever make.

The ultimate decision-making tool is the leading of the Holy Spirit. At the Last Supper, Jesus revealed to his disciples that he was going to the Father but would send "another Counselor." Imagine their confusion! *Another* counselor? How could anyone possibly replace Jesus, their living, breathing, walking friend who had taught them and guided them with such clarity? Jesus calmed their fears by saying,

> I tell you the truth: It is for your good that I am going away. Unless I go away, the Counselor will not come to you; but if I go, I will send him to you. When he comes, he will convict the world of guilt in regard to sin and righteousness and judgment (John 16:7-8).

The second chapter of Acts records the coming of the Holy Spirit as promised, and Christians have been blessed by his supernatural guidance ever since.

Dad, before they reach the age of reason, keep making and modeling wise decisions for your kids. As soon as possible, though, turn it over to the Father, Son, and Holy Spirit. Feel free to stick around as a clarifying force and sounding board as your kids continue in the process of sanctification, but give them plenty of room to practice and hone the skill of decision-making.

They need to be able to discern right from wrong and better from best. For their first thousand choices, they're going to need you as their safety net.

Oh yeah. God also provides access to other decision-making tools as well. The Bible. Prayer. Pastors and elders. Accountability partners. Small groups. A wife of noble character. Teach your kids to use them all. And like so many of the lessons you teach your kids, remember that all these same truths apply to your life as well.

Takeaway

Sometimes dads forget that our ultimate goal is to make ourselves obsolete—to work our way out of a job.

"One father is more than a hundred schoolmasters."
—George Herbert (1593–1633)

52

Kids Need Their Dad...

To Not Confuse
Heritage with Legacy

For most of human history, a father's career choice was passed on from one generation to the next. Why do you think last names like Carpenter, Hunter, Cooper, and Smith are so common? If a father shoveled manure, a young lad didn't have much choice. He received that calling as a heritage and would surely pass it on as his legacy. That, in a nutshell, is the blessing and curse of being part of a family.

These days more than ever, heritage and legacy go far beyond what a person does for a living. You may or may not pass your plumbing business on to your son or your passion for teaching on to your daughter, but the more crucial parts of your legacy actually run deeper than vocation. Integrity begets integrity. Abuse begets abuse. Bigotry begets bigotry. Knowledge-seekers beget knowledge-seekers. A creative spark begets a creative spark. Etcetera.

Certainly there are exceptions. You can choose to say "This character flaw stops with me." Just being aware of the concept of heritage and legacy will help you pass on the best and lay aside the rest. Most of us have plenty of poisonous traits we don't want to pass on to the next generation. The seventeenth-century English philosopher John Locke said, "Parents wonder why the streams are bitter, when they themselves have poisoned the fountain."

So what heritage did you receive from your father? You may have enjoyed great quantity and quality time with a dad who challenged you, loved you, disciplined you, and laughed with you. Or you may have barely known him. In either case—or somewhere in between—you need to come to grips with that relationship. Express thankfulness for all his efforts on your behalf. If possible, continue to invest in his life. If necessary, work toward forgiveness. Let go of resentment. Understand that your father (and mother) came into their parenting responsibilities with a heritage from their parents. Recognize the generational chain—and resolve to make the next link stronger and tighter.

If it has not yet been made clear in the past 51 chapters, the most important legacy you can leave is unconditional love. It doesn't matter how much love was poured into you. God has given you an endless supply, and the more you give, the more you get. When a kid brings home straight A's, love them. When a kid spills his milk, love them. When a teenager wrecks the car, scores a touchdown, ignores curfew, gets elected prom queen, mows the grass without being asked, or comes home pregnant, love them.

Maintain high expectations, enforce family rules, provide consequences, hold them accountable, and dare to discipline. But love them through it. Brag to your friends, post their report card on the fridge, keep a scrapbook of their athletic achievements, and buy them ice cream. But make sure they know you love them for who they are and not what they do.

The good news is that our kids give us a fresh chance to leave the world a better place. Humanity's universal quest for immortality is personified in our children. Most of us will never create any museum-quality art or be inducted into any halls of fame. We can have hope in eternal life, but heaven is a reality beyond this world. Your children are your most tangible connection to the future here on earth. They are your greatest gift to tomorrow, Dad.

The past, present, and future come together right here, right now. Don't miss the power of this turning point in time. Your heritage has been defined by others. It has limits and liabilities. But your legacy remains undefined. It has no limits. It only has potential.

Takeaway

Dad, it's not about you. You can't give your kids everything they need anyway. It's about being there, doing the best you can, loving them with all your heart, and then surrendering their lives back to the Creator.

"He will turn the hearts of the fathers to their children,
and the hearts of the children to their fathers."

—MALACHI 4:6

Blogs and More

The Internet can be a valuable resource for dads of all ages. Below is a list of a few blogs and weekly e-mails you might find useful. (Of course, once you start clicking from Web site to Web site, you'll eventually land on images and ideas that are not family- or father-friendly. Content on these and other links may not be endorsed by the author or the publisher.)

Fathering: Off the Air
John Fuller
johnfullerblog.com/category/fathering

Father Power
Jamie Bohnett
bohnettmemorial.blogspot.com

Wisdom for Divorced Parents
Len Stauffenger
wisdomfordivorcedparents.com/blog

Better Dads
Rick Johnson
authorrickjohnson.blogspot.com

Todd Wilson
Family Man Ministries
Familymanweb.com

A Dad's Point of View
Bruce Sallan
brucesallan.com

Who's Your Daddy?
Michael Bennie
whosyourdaddydiary.blogspot.com

Fathers.com Weekly Inbox
Weekly e-mail
dads@fathers.com

Fathers52: a weekly blog for dads
Jay Payleitner
fathers52.com

Acknowledgments

You can't be a dad in a vacuum. As much as I love helping other dads, I have more frequently been on the receiving end of all kinds of invaluable fathering insight and guidance. Sometimes by direct give-and-take. Sometimes by watching and learning.

My bride, Rita, continues to be the love of my life and a faithful partner in this rewarding journey. I can't imagine doing this without her. My own dad modeled outstanding fathering in ways that I didn't even realize until years later. Without knowing it, my brother Mark, father of three wonderful girls, showed me how to connect with my daughter.

My grandfathers, Orlando Mauel and Fritz Payleitner, must have been doing something right—although, in my youth, I didn't fully appreciate the strong legacy they would leave me and my own family.

What an honor it has been working for more than 15 years with the quietly brilliant Brock Griffin at The National Center for Fathering. Partnering with Brock and the gifted leadership team—CEO Carey Casey, President Peter Spokes, and founder Ken Canfield—has exposed me to many layers of research and provoked me to think long and hard about every aspect of being a dad. Every attentive father in the country benefits from that hardworking team in Kansas City, and I have had a ringside seat.

Josh McDowell came into my life at just the right time. His integrity, sense of purpose, and biblical sagacity gave me an inside track to the blessings of fatherhood. Thanks also, Josh, for your challenging foreword to this book.

In my short tenure as the Executive Director of the Illinois Fatherhood Initiative, founder David Hirsch and colleagues gave me a real-life glimpse into the overwhelming problem of fatherlessness and helped solidify my life's calling.

I will always be grateful to those individuals who helped make this book happen, especially my tenacious and encouraging agent, Sandra Bishop of MacGregor Literary. I have been blessed early and often by the multitalented team at Harvest House. Nick Harrison caught the vision from the very start. Paul Gossard tweaked and slashed verbiage with love and care. Marketing and PR savvy from Barb Sherrill, Katie Lane, Karri James, Aaron Dillon, Dave Bartlett, Elizabeth Colclough, and Christianne Debysingh continues to hit all the right targets.

Afraid that I'll leave someone out, I hesitate to begin listing other great dads who have walked beside me on this journey. But my heart tells me to acknowledge guys like Dan Balow, Tim Hollinger, Dan Anderson, Andrew Bee, Tim Sjostrom, Warren Beeh, Larry Stratton, Dennis O'Malley, Scott Kirk, Tim Coleman, Dwight Curran, Eric Nelson, Larry Breeden, Steve Clausen, Jim Nicodem, Eric Rojas, Wayne Shepherd, Bob Tiede, Frank Mercadante, Ed Kramer, John Albright, Pat Miller, Ralph Andrini, Chuck Thomas, Philip Aspegren, Dave George, Phred Hollister, Jim Goodmiller, Ron Preston, Jim Kenney, Terry Sheehan, Chris Black, Ronn Christensen, Mark Salzmann, Len Asquini, Joe Priola, Gary LaGesse, Dave Potter, Curt Berg, Vance Olson, Coyle Schwab, Tim Feeney, Alan Gall, Steve Jeffrey, Mike Franzen, and Terry Schweizer. To be clear, none of these guys are perfect fathers. I've seen many of them through fathering highs and lows. But I have had authentic conversations with each of them about the joy and privilege of being a dad. And they delight in it. Every one of these men encourages me as a dad.

Mostly, though, my best teachers have been my own five kids and daughter-in-law. They have been honest, patient, respectful, loving, appreciative, and ever-present. I love you, Alec, Randall (and Rachel), Max, Isaac, and Rae Anne. Thanks to all!

Notes

1. Fulton County, Georgia, jail populations, Texas Dept. of Corrections, 1992.

2. Warren R. Stanton, Tian P.S. Oci, and Phil A. Silva, "Sociodemographic Characteristics of Adolescent Smokers," *The International Journal of the Addictions* 7 (1994).

3. U.S. Department of Health and Human Services news release, March 26, 1999.

4. Rainbows for All God's Children.

5. Jean Bethke Elshtain, "Family Matters: The Plight of America's Children," *The Christian Century,* July 1993.

6. John O.G. Billy, Karin L. Brewster, and William R. Grady, "Contextual Effects on the Sexual Behavior of Adolescent Women," *Journal of Marriage and Family* 56 (1994).

7. Werner Haug and Phillipe Warner, "The demographic characteristics of the linguistic and religious groups in Switzerland" in vol. 2, *Population Studies,* no. 31, "The demographic characteristics of national minorities in certain European states," *Social Cohesion,* ed. Werner Haug et al. (Strasbourg, France: Council of Europe Directorate General III, 2000), as quoted in "Fathers of the Church," *New Directions,* vol. 5, no. 83 (April 2002).

8. Deirdre O'Reilly, www.nlm.nih.gov/medlineplus/ency/article/001598.htm. O'Reilly is an MD and MPH working as a neonatologist in the Division of Newborn Medicine, Children's Hospital Boston, and as an instructor in pediatrics, Harvard Medical School, Boston, Massachusetts.

9. Anderson M. Rearick III, "Matters of Opinion: Hallowing Halloween," *Christianity Today,* October 2, 2000.

10. W. Bradford Wilcox, "Is Religion an Answer? Marriage, Fatherhood, and the Male Problematic," Research Brief No. 11, June 2008, The Center for Marriage and Families, based at the Institute for American Values. Commissioned by the National Fatherhood Initiative.

About the Author

Jay Payleitner is a dad. But he pays his mortgage and feeds his family working as a freelance writer, ad man, speaker, creativity trainer, and radio producer with credits including *Josh McDowell Radio*, *WordPower*, *Jesus Freaks Radio* and *Today's Father with Carey Casey*. Jay served as the Executive Director for the Illinois Fatherhood Initiative and is a featured writer/blogger for the National Center for Fathering. He is the author of *The One-Year Life Verse Devotional*, *40 Days to Your Best Life for Men*, and the acclaimed modern parable *Once Upon a Tandem*. Jay and his high school sweetheart, Rita, have four sons, one daughter, and one daughter-in-law and live in St. Charles, Illinois. You can read his weekly dadblog at www.fathers52.com.

The National Center for Fathering

We believe *every* child needs a dad they can count on. At the National Center for Fathering, we inspire and equip men to be the involved fathers, stepfathers, grandfathers, and father figures their children need.

The National Center was founded by Dr. Ken Canfield in 1990 as a nonprofit scientific and education organization. Today, under the leadership of CEO Carey Casey, we continue to provide practical, research-based training and resources that reach more than one million dads annually.

We focus our work in four areas, all of which are described in detail at fathers.com:

Research. The Personal Fathering Profile, developed by a team of researchers led by Ken Canfield, and other ongoing research projects provide fresh insights for fathers and serve as benchmarks for evaluating the effectiveness of our programs and resources.

Training. Through Championship Fathering Experiences, Father-Daughter Summits, online training, small-group curricula, and train-the-trainer programs, we have equipped over 80,000 fathers and more than 1000 trainers to impact their own families and local communities.

Programs. The National Center provides leading edge, turnkey fathering programs, including WATCH D.O.G.S. (Dads Of Great Students), which involves dads in their children's education and is currently in more than 1300 schools in 36 states. Other programs include Fathering Court, which helps dads with significant child-support arrearages, and our annual Father of the Year Essay Contest.

Resources. Our Web site provides a wealth of resources for dads in nearly every fathering situation, many of them available free of charge. Dads who make a commitment to Championship Fathering receive a free weekly e-newsletter full of timely and practical tips on fathering. *Today's Father*, Carey Casey's daily radio program, airs on 600-plus stations. Listen to programs online or download podcasts at fathers.com/radio.

Make your commitment to Championship Fathering

Championship Fathering is an effort to change the culture for today's children and the children of coming generations. We're seeking to reach, teach, and unleash 6.5 million dads, creating a national movement of men who will commit to LOVE their children, COACH their children, MODEL for their children, ENCOURAGE other children, and ENLIST other dads to join the team. To make the Championship Fathering commitment, visit fathers.com/cf.
